OUT OF DARKNESS
AND INTO
CHRIST

RENE PELLEYA-KOURI, M.D.

with Cheryl Williams

Order this book online at www.trafford.com
or email orders@trafford.com

Most Trafford titles are also available at major online book retailers.

Cover art by: Virginia Vega

Unless otherwise noted; scripture quotations are taken from:

Scripture quotations marked NKJV are taken from the New King James Version.
Copyright © 1982 by Thomas Nelson, Inc. Used by permission. All rights reserved.

Scripture quotations marked NIV are taken from the *Holy Bible, New International
Version*®. *NIV*®. Copyright © 1973, 1978, 1984 by International Bible Society.
Used by permission of Zondervan. All rights reserved. [Biblica]

Scripture quotations marked AMP are from *The Amplified Bible*, Old Testament copyright ©
1965, 1987 by the Zondervan Corporation. *The Amplified Bible*, New Testament copyright ©
1954, 1958, 1987 by The Lockman Foundation. Used by permission. All rights reserved.

Print information available on the last page.

ISBN: 978-1-4907-6720-8 (sc)
ISBN: 978-1-4907-6722-2 (hc)
ISBN: 978-1-4907-6721-5 (e)

Library of Congress Control Number: 2015919708

Trafford rev. 12/19/2015

www.trafford.com
North America & international
toll-free: 1 888 232 4444 (USA & Canada)
fax: 812 355 4082

TABLE OF CONTENTS

ACKNOWLEDGMENTS

To God
Father, Son and Holy Spirit
I love You so much.
To my partner in this book, Cheryl Williams and her husband, Dwight. Thank you for your help, encouragement, guidance, instructions, and blessings.
To my wonderful wife, Betty who blesses me 24/7, thank you so much.
To my children, Cristina and Lacy, and my grandchildren, Lucas and Isabel.
To Betty's children, Carlos and Cristina.
To Maria, my sister, who always pushes us higher.
To Fifi, and all the extended family.
To my in laws.
To our Love and Fire group, keep fanning the flame.
To all the saints that minister to us.
To our place of work, city and great nation.
To Tanzania's Agape Center and Don Bosco Orphanage.
To Helen and Lauren, who typed and edited the manuscript.
To our overseers, Frank Marzullo, Cheryl Williams, Maria Vadia, and Rosario Garrido.
May the Lord bless you and keep you.
The Lord make His face to shine upon you and be gracious to you.
The Lord lift up His countenance upon you and give you peace.
So they shall put My name on the children of Israel and I will bless them.
Amen.

CHAPTER ONE
"INTRODUCTION"

The Kingdom Increases!

> *Daniel 2:44 – And in the days of these kings the God of heaven will set up a kingdom which shall never be destroyed; and the kingdom shall not be left to other people; it shall break in pieces and consume all these kingdoms, and it shall stand forever.*

> *Psalm 145:13 - Your kingdom is an everlasting kingdom, And Your dominion endures throughout all generations.*

Since my last book, "Praying Doctors: Jesus in the Office", I have been to Africa five times, as well as to Europe and South America. After seven years of total celibacy, the Lord gave me a most wonderful woman, Jesus lover and a powerful intercessor. We have a blessed home ministry, with teaching, equipping, healing and Impartation. We are connected to an orphanage in Tanzania, Wattoto Wetu Tanzania / Friends of Don Bosco, where we of course, donate money. Many of the "orphans" are now saved, healed and delivered as well as empowered with the Holy Spirit. They are healing the sick and casting out devils. We are also connected with Agape Center at Dar Es Salaam, a Catholic, charismatic healing and deliverance center, where we are invited to minister healing crusades with miracle signs and wonders.

God is still in the business of miracles!

At the same time that we are receiving such blessings, we are in the midst of warfare.

Even before I was saved, I had a desire to help the sick and wounded. I myself, lived most of my life sick, wounded and imprisoned. I spent dozens of years in the kingdom of darkness investigating every possible way to heal others and myself. I was on a downward spiral, a course filled with many crashes: addictions, destruction, grief, and loss.

My God, I made it only because of You.

When the Holy Spirit filled me and came upon me, I underwent many months of repenting, renouncing, forgiving, cleansing and deliverance. God absolutely rescued me from hell.

I was never into "religion," so soon God began to act powerfully in my life, in my inner life and in my ministry.

I had been involved in Shamanic practices of Imagery and Visualization where we would invite animal guides to take us through journeys. The counterfeit power comes as an angel of light.

I was convinced that this power was from God. My whole life was dedicated to my relationship with these "beings". They provided "all I needed" for my healing and to guide others into their healing. Truthfully, though, my life progressively deteriorated.

God healed me instantly from cocaine addiction by a pond in Mississippi in 1983 – I had reached absolute rock bottom and called upon His name. With this healing, I had no foundation upon which to stand. I could not believe that the powerful God that healed me was attached to a church. I had judged the denominational churches as dry and impotent, so I went into other religions that promised I would find God.

When I surrendered to the Holy Spirit in 2003, the power of seeing that I had acquired through the Shamanic practices was absolutely taken away from me. I was bewildered. I didn't understand.

Because I was a physician, I even considered that I had suffered a stroke in some inner vision areas. I depended so much on such visions, but God spoke to me and said, "I took it away, I did not give it to you. It came from the wrong source. I know what is best for you.". I felt such love. I wept for a long time. I became blind to my old source of power. I was to depend only on Him. A year later, while in a Prophetic School where they were activating the Seer area, the leader asked us to invite an animal that would be symbolic of a certain process that we were going through. I reacted strongly to such suggestions. God had taken away such animal imagery! The leader said this was sanctified, our Father would give us good things. I finally agreed. We were under the Holy Spirit. Immediately, I saw an eagle. I had met that eagle before. I knew that it wanted to exalt itself above the knowledge of God. I was disturbed.

I began to powerfully praise the Lord as in Psalm 149. In this place, the most remarkable thing happened. I saw a sword coming from above, out of the mouth of a child, that totally destroyed that eagle. As I kept praising, I saw a new eagle, a different eagle coming out of the river of God. The eagle just praised the Lord. I was aghast with these visions. I had a revelation of the two Kingdoms, and a deep knowledge of the counterfeit. One eagle was demonic - it exalted itself above the knowledge of God, the other eagle was from God, it always praised Him.

I began to build a powerful trust in God. Slowly God gave me visions, dreams and the prophetic gift. It was definitely different from previously, not long journeys, but short pieces of information that through faith would develop. This difference is manifest, especially when I am to minister, He puts thoughts into my mind of what I am to do, what is going to happen and that is so awesome and powerful! *Thank you Lord.*

In my unsaved life, I worked for the discovery of hidden wounds and ways to heal them. In 1983, God in all his sovereignty, took away my cocaine addiction in a moment.

I received Him as Lord and Savior at my mother's funeral in 2002. In 2003, the Holy Spirit filled me and in a moment totally took away my sex addiction. I was absolutely delivered and freed from sexual bondage and stayed alone for seven years, for the first time in my life since the age of 13!!

So I experienced the One Step program, but I also recognized the "12 Step Program" of progressive sanctification. The Scripture says that we who are in Christ are a new creation and that the old life passed away. We absolutely need transformation through the renewal of our minds to grasp that truth and somehow it appears that we need to fight for our salvation - sanctification with fear and trembling.

Our healing and deliverance is a progressive <u>PROCESS</u> in which it is not only the healing of an issue, but revelation with which we help others. I call this process 'painful productions'.

- Revelation of the love of God
- Learning to soak and wait for His presence
- Intimacy
- Character formation
- Humility
- Recognition of the wiles of the devil
- Learning about the fellowship of His suffering

Every morning I set a minimum of two hours before I go to work where I lay down on my prayer sofa and look for Him. I just love Him and pray to love Him more and pray to be able to receive more of His love. Anything can happen in my mornings with Him. At times I just abide in His love. At other times a healing and deliverance and a teaching comes forth.

Most of this book came from such connection with my Lord Jesus. I have used it in my weekly teachings and our prayer team has received tremendous blessings, healing, deliverance and impartations. So I pray that the windows of Heaven open to you to receive all blessings from Heavenly places. I pray that the eyes of your heart open to see, perceive, hear, and know the deep knowledge of Christ, your hope of glory.

I pray that as you grow experientially through this book, you receive a greater degree of healing, deliverance and impartation.

I pray for a new mantle to fall upon you as you raise holy hands. But above all, I pray that the Holy Spirit releases anew the love of Christ into your hearts, the love that never fails, the love that abides in you forever.

God is love. *Thank you Father! Thank you Jesus! Thank you Holy Spirit!*

CHAPTER TWO
"EXPLANATION"

Out of the Darkness: Concerning Our Identity

Without an awareness of our identity in Christ, we are operating in a darkness, which cripples us and hinders the effectiveness of our ministry to the kingdom of God. We who are in Christ, have the Holy Spirit and are established in His Victory on the cross.

The purpose of this book is to reveal to ministers and lay people alike the power and authority given us, as we are children of the light. Once we have appropriated the Victory Jesus achieved at the Cross we can minister this freedom to others.

At the cross, Jesus disarmed principalities and powers and made a spectacle of them. When we live in the light of this victory, we are no longer held captive by the darkness our enemy spreads, keeping us hostage to fear, defeat, lying, etc.

We begin our study with Jehovah Nissi, God is our Banner, God is our Victory. Generally, the saints have hidden unresolved issues, unsaved areas in us, persistent hurts, wounds, reactions to wounds and unholy fruit.

We are calling these things that persist, <u>strongholds</u>. This book invites us to go deep, uncovering such holdouts of the devil and destroying them so we can appropriate the fullness of the Blessings already released from our God.

A main purpose of this book is to familiarize the people of God with the wiles of the devil in these areas and to activate the ministry of deliverance and self-deliverance necessary for the freedom of us all.

Case Study

Tonya, exhibiting **A stronghold of bitterness**

Tonya and her husband came to see me. These were Holy Spirit filled Christians that seemed to have a place of oppression and strife. They were both anointed ministers in love with the Lord and dedicated to ministering to lost and wounded souls. The man had been to Christian Healing Ministries where he underwent major healing and deliverance of multiple issues.

Tonya after many years of being born again, began to realize that there were hidden, unhealed, issues still affecting her life. She was very loving and most people were attracted to her demeanor and wonderful presence. Tonya's husband really loved her and supported her, but he believed that there were hidden issues behind her wonderful facade and personality.

He thought that somehow Tonya was transferring into him some unresolved issues such as anger and bitterness and he occasionally reacted in such a way and he could not find any reason for such behavior.

Tonya agreed that he was feeling what she had, but that she never specifically addressed it, nor could she conquer it all with the Word, praise and worship, speaking in tongues. The feeling would abate, but it would always return.

As the Bible states, married couples are one flesh so I really think that unfinished business, un-worked issues, hidden things, unhealed wounds, demons can be transferred, so I was willing to investigate such possibility of transference.

We asked the Holy Spirit to open a window, for the purpose of 'seeing' into her issues and so I dealt with Tonya. We investigated hidden places in the soul:

> Judgment of her mother
>
> Totally hidden and transferred to husband
>
> Husband was feeling anger that he could not explain
> Bitterness DEFILES others!

This is a 'no, no' for many Christians for many reasons i.e.: psychology, the new age, etc, but we have the Spirit of Truth to uncover hidden things of darkness. We are the lamp of the Lord, that searches. We need to lay the ax to the root.

I believe that we need to go deeper from our conscious, intellectual, even superficial minds like David said, "Search my Heart, even hidden sin" (Psalm 139:3), (Psalm 90:8), (Psalm 19:12, 13). So sin can be hidden and continue to hurt us and cause dysfunction in our lives.

We first called upon the Holy Spirit that He would guide us into the heart of the matter, the hidden roots, so we asked the Holy Spirit to take Tonya inwards...

In her mind's eye, in her sanctified spiritual perception, she saw herself as an adolescent, 14 years old (Now she was 61 years old), watching her mother in a car kissing a man. Tonya saw the adolescent and felt her reaction. Shock, hurt, deep rejection, judgment, anger, rage, wrath, blame, condemnation. At that moment she began to hate her mother and rebel.

For many years she led a rebellious life of sexual immorality and drug addiction; when she was 21 years old, she received Jesus Christ as Lord and Savior and her life was totally changed. She stopped drugs, got married, had children, and was successful at her work, but something hurtful and damaging persisted inside.

She never again could bond with her mother and the same happened between Tonya and her daughter. She had no idea why this could be happening; she had totally put away from her thoughts and repressed this event. Now the Holy Spirit was taking her to that deep place of wounding (when she saw her mother kissing a strange man) and her reactions to such a wound.

Sins manifested within this stronghold

A) Judgment

Matthew 7:1 – *Judge not, that you be not judged.*

Romans 2:1 – *Therefore you are inexcusable, O man, whoever you are who judge, for in whatever you judge another you condemn yourself; for you who judge practice the same things.*

B) Thoughts/Behaviors Dishonoring her mother

Exodus 20:12 – *Honor your father and your mother, that your days may be long upon the land which the LORD your God is giving you.*

Matthew 15:4 – *For God commanded,   saying, 'Honor your father and your mother'; and, 'He who curses father or mother, let him be put to death.'*

C) Unforgiveness

The Parable of the Unforgiving Servant,

> Matthew 18:21-35 – *Then Peter came to Him and said, "Lord, how often shall my brother sin against me, and I forgive him? Up to seven times?" Jesus said to him, "I do not say to you, up*

to seven times, but up to seventy times seven. Therefore the kingdom of heaven is like a certain king who wanted to settle accounts with his servants. And when he had begun to settle accounts, one was brought to him who owed him ten thousand talents. But as he was not able to pay, his master commanded that he be sold, with his wife and children and all that he had, and that payment be made. The servant therefore fell down before him, saying, 'Master, have patience with me, and I will pay you all.' Then the master of that servant was moved with compassion, released him, and forgave him the debt.

"But that servant went out and found one of his fellow servants who owed him a hundred denarii; and he laid hands on him and took him by the throat, saying, 'Pay me what you owe!' So his fellow servant fell down at his feet and begged him, saying, 'Have patience with me, and I will pay you all. And he would not, but went and threw him into prison till he should pay the debt.

So when his fellow servants saw what had been done, they were very grieved, and came and told their master all that had been done. Then his master, after he had called him, said to him, 'You wicked servant! I forgave you all that debt because you begged me. Should you not also have had compassion on your fellow servant, just as I had pity on you?' And his master was angry, and delivered him to the torturers until he should pay all that was due to him

"So My heavenly Father also will do to you if each of you, from his heart, does not forgive his brother his trespasses."

Mark 11:25 – *And whenever you stand praying, if you have anything against anyone, forgive him, that your Father in heaven may also forgive you your trespasses.*

Taking Steps to Freedom

1) Break strongholds of bitterness

Hebrews 12:15 – *Looking carefully lest anyone fall short of the grace of God; lest any root of bitterness springing up cause trouble, and by this many become defiled;*

2) Dig deep

Luke 6:48 – *He is like a man building a house who dug deep and laid the foundation on the rock. And when the flood arose, the stream beat vehemently against that house, and could not shake it, for it was founded on the rock.*

Matthew 3:10- *And even now the ax is laid to the root of the trees. Therefore every tree which does not bear good fruit is cut down and thrown into the fire.*

At that session, when she was seeing the adolescent girl, I felt directed by the Holy Spirit to suggest that Tonya should talk to her mother. I believe that this was a disowned part of Tonya that was just put away. I believe we do this. I have found in many counseling sessions that there are hidden parts of my clients, even some who hate their "inner child."

Why? The parents might have judged them, treated them unfairly, there is a blame and condemnation system against the child and as these people have grown up, they themselves have become part of the self-accusing system = self-hatred.

Steps to Maintain Freedom

We have the ministry of reconciliation, even inner reconciliation. What is God's law:

1. Love God
2. Love our neighbor as ourselves, as we love ourselves

I believe we are called to love our whole self, so I believe that Christians guided, by the Holy Spirit, ought to investigate hidden, forgotten places of hurt. Yes, we have all been hurt and many of us have repressed memories, places that act out, unhealed places that act out and defile.

Hebrews 12:15 - *Looking carefully lest anyone fall short of the grace of God; lest any root of bitterness springing up cause trouble, and by this many become defiled;*

Unhealed places can be transferred onto others, emotions can be transferred, evil spirits that infect emotions can be transferred and all these need healing and deliverance.

In the case of Tonya, the Holy Spirit took her to her adolescent years, 47 years earlier! Something that she had put away, but was still affecting her in many ways.

With her mother
With her daughter
With her husband
With herself

This was an unhealed wound, a festering area of unforgiveness, judgment, bitterness, resentment, and separation, even an open door for demonic influence.
"If you don't forgive, I send you to the tormentors. If you don't forgive, I will not forgive you. If you judge, you will be judged. If you judge, you are going to do the same thing."

Tonya wept realizing this inner dysfunction. There was a deep sadness. She saw how her adolescent reacted to the situation with rebellion. She also realized that there was a prevalent state of shame.

The Power of The Lord, Our Healer

We invited our Lord Jesus into that place of captivity. She saw Him holding her and the adolescent. The young woman wept as they received the healing that only Jesus brings.

Tonya went and met with her mother and shared the whole event. They both wept, there was honesty and a new heart to heart connection rose up. Tonya did the same with her daughter. There was healing of the wounds of the generations.

Isaiah 61:4 – *And they shall rebuild the old ruins, They shall raise up the former desolations, And they shall repair the ruined cities, The desolations of many generations.*

Listen, we are always wildly praising our God, we are always into the Word, and we speak in tongues at all times. We are into transformation by renewal of our minds. We realize our true victorious identity in Christ and I truly believe that at times the Lord wants us to be still and visit hidden places of captivity in us where He wants to bring His Sozo, meaning total salvation healing and deliverance.

He is a God of wholeness! Thank you Lord!

w{

CHAPTER THREE
"JEHOVA NISSI"

We have learned by studying Scripture to appropriate the victory intended for us by Our God. Follow along and witness God's plan of victory for Moses, as he led the children of Israel through the wilderness. Learn the faithfulness of Our God to Joshua when the responsibility of leadership was handed to him.

"But that was Then," you may protest. Oh, yes, you are so right in your observation. Witness the persistence of your enemy as the Amalekites rise up again, and know that Our God is the Everlasting God. There is none like Him. He has destined us to victory, even before the foundation of the world. The plan and purposes of Jehovah Nissi are Eternal, as He is Eternal. Read on.

Moses' Calling and Jehovah's Protection

Exodus 3:1 – Now Moses was tending the flock of Jethro, his father-in-law, the priest of Midian, and he led the flock to the back of the desert, and came to Horeb, the mountain of God.

V2 And the Angel of the LORD appeared to him in a flame of fire from the midst of a bush. So he looked, and behold, the bush was burning with fire, but the bush was *not* consumed.

V4 So when the LORD saw that he turned aside to look, God called to him from the midst of the bush and said, "Moses, Moses!"

And he said, "Here I am."

V7 And the LORD said: "I have surely seen the oppression of My people who *are* in Egypt, and have heard their cry because of their taskmasters, for I know their sorrows.

V8 So I have come down to deliver them out of the hand of the Egyptians, and to bring them up from that land to a good and large land, to a land flowing with milk and honey, to the place of the Canaanites and the Hittites and the Amorites and the Perizzites and the Hivites and the Jebusites.

Exodus 4:17 And you shall take this rod in your hand, with which you shall do the signs.

V20 Then Moses took his wife and his sons and set them on a donkey, and he returned to the land of Egypt. And Moses took the rod of God in his hand.

Exodus 14:13 – And Moses said to the people, "Do not be afraid. Stand still, and see the salvation of the LORD, which He will accomplish for you today. For the Egyptians whom you see today, you shall see again no more forever.

V14 The Lord will fight for you, and you shall hold your peace.

V16 But lift up your rod, and stretch out your hand over the sea and divide it. And the children of Israel shall go on dry *ground* through the midst of the sea.

Exodus 15: The Song of Moses
Sing or pray it out loud. Declare it!

V1 Then Moses and the children of Israel sang this song to the
LORD, and spoke, saying:
"I will sing to the LORD,
For He has triumphed gloriously!
The horse and its rider
He has thrown into the sea!
V2 The LORD *is* my strength and song,
And He has become my salvation;
He *is* my God, and I will praise Him;
My father's God, and I will exalt Him.

V3 The LORD *is* a man of war;
The LORD *is* His name.

V6 "Your right hand, O LORD, has become glorious in power;
our right hand, O LORD, has dashed the enemy in pieces.

V11 "Who *is* like You, O LORD, among the gods?
Who *is* like You, glorious in holiness,
Fearful in praises, doing wonders?

V13 You in Your mercy have led forth
The people whom You have redeemed;
You have guided *them* in Your strength
To Your holy habitation.

V17 You will bring them in and plant them
In the mountain of Your inheritance,
In the place, O LORD, *which* You have made
For Your own dwelling,
The sanctuary, O Lord, *which* Your hands have established.

V18 "The LORD shall reign forever and ever."

Bitter waters made sweet

Note the acts of obedience called for and the promise God made to His children, even as He identified Himself!

Exodus 15:23 – Now when they came to Marah, they could not drink the waters of Marah, for they were bitter. Therefore the name of it was called Marah.

V25 So he cried out to the LORD, and the LORD showed him a tree. When he cast *it* into the waters, the waters were made sweet. There He made a statute and an ordinance for them, and there He tested them

V26 and said, "If you diligently heed the voice of the LORD your God and do what is right in His sight, give ear to His commandments and keep all His statutes, I will put none of the diseases on you which I have brought on the Egyptians. For I *am* the LORD who heals you."

V27 Then they came to Elim, where there were twelve wells of water and seventy palm trees, so they camped there by the waters.

Victory over the Amalekites
Joshua fights, Moses holds the Victory

Exodus 17:8 –Now Amalek came and fought with Israel in Rephidim.

V9 And Moses said to Joshua, "Choose us some men and go out, fight with Amalek. Tomorrow I will stand on the top of the hill with the rod of God in my hand."

V10 So Joshua did as Moses said to him, and fought with Amalek. And Moses, Aaron, and Hur went up to the top of the hill.

V11 And so it was, when Moses held up his hand, that Israel prevailed; and when he let down his hand, Amalek prevailed.

V12 But Moses' hands *became* heavy; so they took a stone and put *it* under him, and he sat on it. And Aaron and Hur supported his hands, one on one side, and the other on the other side; and his hands were steady until the going down of the sun.

V13 So Joshua defeated Amalek and his people with the edge of the sword.

V14 Then the LORD said to Moses, "Write this *for* a memorial in the book and recount *it* in the hearing of Joshua, that I will utterly blot out the remembrance of Amalek from under heaven."

V15 And Moses built an altar and called its name, <u>The-LORD-Is-My-Banner</u>

V16 for he said, "Because the LORD has sworn: the LORD *will have* war with Amalek from generation to generation."

There is a spiritual war still being fought today. Amalek is a biblical representation of the devil's hostility toward Christ and His body on Earth, a war between Heaven and Hell, a perpetual conflict waged against God by the principalities and powers of Hell.

The Amalakites continued to rise up.

Numbers 14:45 – Then the Amalekites and the Canaanites who dwelt in that mountain came down and attacked them, and drove them back as far as Hormah.

In 1 Samuel 15, Saul's disobedience in sparing Agag, king of the Amalekites, cost him his crown. Later in 2 Samuel 1 an Amalekite finished him off.

In 1 Samuel 30 we see how the Amalekites invaded David's stronghold at Ziklag.

In Esther 3, Haman, an Amalekite, attempted to destroy the Israelites.

The War Continues
And this time, YOU hold the Victory!

The spirit that possessed the Amalekites continues to torment God's people. Observe these instructions given to encourage us in the battle.

1 Peter 5:8 – Be sober, be vigilant, because our adversary the devil walks about like a roaring lion, seeking whom he may devour

In his 1 Corinthians 10, the Apostle Paul gives us leadership and encouragement for victory in the spirit realm:

A) We are in a war
    Ephesians 6:12 - *For we do not wrestle against flesh and blood, but against principalities, against powers, against the rulers of the darkness of this age, against spiritual hosts of wickedness in the heavenly places*

B) When we get attacked the Redeemer of Zion will give us the victory
    Isaiah 59:16-21.
    Let God arise and His enemies be scattered Psalm 68:1

C) The Lord gives us constant reminders of His involvement in the battle WITH us: Jesus, our High Priest, The Cross, The Rod
    Exodus 17:13 – *So Joshua defeated Amalek and his people with the edge of the sword.*
    1 Corinthians 1:18 – *For the message of the cross is foolishness to those who are perishing, but to us who are being saved it is the power of God.*

Exodus 17:15,16 – *And Moses built an altar and called its name, The-LORD-Is-My-Banner; for he said, "Because the LORD has sworn: the LORD will have war with Amalek from generation to generation."*

Isaiah 11:1-5 – *There shall come forth a Rod from the stem of Jesse,*

And a Branch shall grow out of his roots.
V2 *The Spirit of the LORD shall rest upon Him,*
     The Spirit of wisdom and understanding,
     The Spirit of counsel and might,
     The Spirit of knowledge and of the fear of the LORD.

V3 *His delight is in the fear of the LORD,*
     And He shall not judge by the sight of His eyes,
     Nor decide by the hearing of His ears;

V4 *But with righteousness He shall judge the poor, And decide with equity for the meek of the earth; He shall strike the earth with the rod of His mouth,*
     And with the breath of His lips He shall slay the *wicked.*

V5 *Righteousness shall be the belt of His loins,*
     And faithfulness the belt of His waist.
     Always look to Jehova Nissi, our victory. Jesus' victory on the cross was complete, but we are still engaged in warfare. The devil wars against Christ in us. We are Christ's heritage.

Deuteronomy 20:3 – *And he shall say to them, 'Hear, O Israel: Today you are on the verge of battle with your enemies. Do not let your heart faint, do not be afraid, and do not tremble or be terrified because of them;*

V4 *for the LORD your God is He who goes with you, to fight for you against your enemies, to save you.'*

Hebrews 7:24 – *But He, because He continues forever, has an unchangeable priesthood.*

V25 *Therefore He is also able to save to the uttermost those who come to God through Him, since He always lives to make intercession for them.*

V26 *For such a High Priest was fitting for us, who is holy, harmless, undefiled, separate from sinners, and has become higher than the heavens;*

John 17 – *Jesus spoke these words, lifted up His eyes to heaven, and said: "Father, the hour has come. Glorify Your Son, that Your Son also may glorify You,*

V9 *"I pray for them. I do not pray for the world but for those whom You have given Me, for they are Yours.*

V11 *Now I am no longer in the world, but these are in the world, and I come to You. Holy Father, keep through Your name those whom You have given Me that they may be one as We are.*

V12 *While I was with them in the world, I kept them in Your name. Those whom You gave Me I have kept; and none of them is lost except the son of perdition, that the Scripture might be fulfilled.*

V15 *I do not pray that You should take them out of the world, but that You should keep them from the evil one.*

Romans 8 – *God's everlasting love*

V31 *What then shall we say to these things? If God is for us, who can be against us?*

V32 *He who did not spare His own Son, but delivered Him up for us all, how shall He not with Him also freely give us all things?*

V33 *Who shall bring a charge against God's elect? It is God who justifies.*

V34 *Who is he who condemns? It is Christ who died, and furthermore is also risen, who is even at the right hand of God, who also makes intercession for us.*

V35 *Who shall separate us from the love of Christ? Shall tribulation, or distress, or persecution, or famine, or nakedness, or peril, or sword?*

V36 *As it is written:*
   "For Your sake we are killed all day long;
   We are accounted as sheep for the slaughter."

V37 *Yet in all these things we are more than conquerors through Him who loved us.*

V38 *For I am persuaded that neither death nor life, nor angels nor principalities nor powers, nor things present nor things to come,*

V39 *nor height nor depth, nor any other created thing, shall be able to separate us from the love of God which is in Christ Jesus our Lord.*

1 Corinthians 13:8 *Love never fails*

Isaiah 59:19 – *When the enemy comes in like a flood, the Spirit of the Lord will lift up a standard against him.*

Isaiah 54:17 – *No weapon formed against you shall prosper, And every tongue which rises against you in judgment you shall condemn. This is the heritage of the servants of the LORD,*
   And their righteousness is from Me,"
   Says the LORD.

Armed with these scriptures, and His assurance of victory as you battle, follow these instructions:

Pray out loud against the enemy in this manner:

Declare the name of your enemy.
Rejection you are crushed.
Fear you are defeated.
Poverty be gone.
Addiction you have ended.
Curses you are broken.
Diseases this is your end.
Whatever has come in like a flood, stop it!
Declare its demise.
We have a standard.
We have a banner.
We have Jehova Nissi.
We have Jehova our Victory.
We have the Rod.
We have Jesus the Lord of Lords. We have the cross.
Thank you Lord.

Prayer for Victory

Thank you Lord that because of your blood, body, death, resurrection, ascension and coronation, I have been saved, healed, delivered, redeemed, sanctified, justified, set apart for you. Thank you Lord that you gave us all authority and power over the power of the enemy. Thank you Lord that you gave us the power of decree. We decree today our victory in Christ over sin, disease, infirmities, afflictions: physical, emotional, mental and spiritual, poverty, curses, evil spirits and whatever is not of You.

Thank you Lord that in the cross You said "it is finished". Today, by faith, I appropriate my victory in Christ and declare once again, I am more than a conqueror through Jesus Christ who loves me.

Amen.

Thank You Lord.

$\sqrt{}$

CHAPTER FOUR
"HEALING THROUGH DELIVERANCE"

Key scripture Luke 10:19- *Behold, I give you the authority to trample on serpents and scorpions, and over all the power of the enemy, and nothing shall by any means hurt you.*

In this chapter we will deal with deliverance in general. There are whole books [2,3,4,5] on the subject. We will explain how we cast out demons as a natural occurrence in our ministry.

Definition

Deliverance – the process of expelling demons. To set free from evil. To rescue from bondage.

In His first sermon, in Luke 4:18, where He read Isaiah 61, Jesus said: *"The Spirit of the Lord is on me, because he has anointed me to preach the gospel to the poor. He has sent me to heal the brokenhearted, To **proclaim liberty** to the captives; And recovery of sight to the blind, To set at **liberty those who are oppressed**.*

In Acts 10:38, *Peter preached to Cornelius and said how God anointed Jesus of Nazareth with the Holy Spirit and with power, who went about doing good and healing all who were* **oppressed by the devil**, *for God was with Him.*

The first thing Jesus did after He began His ministry was to cast out a **devil** at a synagogue (Luke 4:35).

Mark 7:25-30 *For a woman whose young daughter had an* **unclean spirit** *heard about Him, and she came and fell at His feet.*

V26 *The woman was a Greek, a Syro-Phoenician by birth, and she kept asking Him to cast the* **demon** *out of her daughter.*

V27 *But Jesus said to her, "Let the children be filled first, for it is not good to take the children's bread and throw it to the little dogs."*

V28 And she answered and said to Him, "Yes, Lord, yet even the little dogs under the table eat from the children's crumbs."

V29 *Then He said to her, "For this saying go your way; the* **demon** *has gone out of your daughter."*

V30 *And when she had come to her house, she found the* **demon** *gone out, and her daughter lying on the bed.*

Jesus called **deliverance** the children's bread. He did it everywhere, at church, in the streets, and in the marketplace.

Psalm 107:20 – *He sent His word and healed them, And* **delivered** *them from their destructions.*

What are demons? Are demons real? Look at Jesus' ministry. He said in John 14:12 that we would do the same that He did and even more! The apostles cast out demons.

There are certain types of demons: earthbound spirits with all the characteristics of a person – will, intellect, emotions, speech.

Matt 12:43-45 refers to <u>the earthbound demons</u> that can inhabit people.

In Daniel 10, we see another kind of supernatural spiritual being – angels fighting in the heavens (the 2nd heaven). The angel that was sent to Daniel called the evil spirit that withstood him 21 days, "the prince of the kingdom of Persia".(the principalities that Paul mentions in Ephesians 6. This type of evil spirit, a fallen angel, seems to be different than the kind that inhabits people.

Ephesians 6:12 points to different kinds of evil beings (principalities, powers, rulers of darkness of this world, spiritual wickedness in high places, (heavenly places).

There seems to be an evil hierarchy, but, we have power over them, through the Covenant of the blood of the Lord Jesus Christ.

1 John 4:4 – *You are of God, little children, and have overcome them, because He who is in you is greater than he who is in the world.*

Luke 10:19 – *Behold, I give you the authority to trample on serpents and scorpions, and over all the power of the enemy, and nothing shall by any means hurt you.*

Colossians 2:13-15 – *And you, being dead in your trespasses and the uncircumcision of your flesh, He has made alive together with Him, having forgiven you all trespasses,*

V14 *having wiped out the handwriting of requirements that was against us, which was contrary to us. And He has taken it out of the way, having nailed it to the cross.*

V15 *Having disarmed principalities and powers, He made a public spectacle of them, triumphing over them in it.*

Philippians 2:9-11 – *Therefore God also has highly exalted Him and given Him the name which is above every name,*

V10 *that at the name of Jesus every knee should bow, of those in heaven, and of those on earth, and of those under the earth,*

V11 *and that every tongue should confess that Jesus Christ is Lord, to the glory of God the Father.*

Romans 8:31 – *What then shall we say to these things? If God is for us, who can be against us?*

James 4:7 – *Therefore submit to God. Resist the devil and he will flee from you.*

Can a Christian have a demon?

Acts 5:3 *But Peter said, "Ananias, why has Satan filled your heart to lie to the Holy Spirit and keep back part of the price of the land for yourself?*

Judas, an apostle, betrayed Jesus.

I was baptized and received confirmation and when the Holy Spirit filled me, many demons came out of me. How do demons come out? We see in Mark 1:23-26 that the demons came out with a loud voice. A demon is a spirit. The Greek word for spirit, pneuma, also means breath. When a demon comes out of a person, it normally comes out through his mouth and there is usually some manifestation like coughing, burping, yawning, spitting, vomiting, yelling.

Entrance doors. How do demons enter?

Entrance doors are closely related to the root causes of illnesses. *

1) Sins of the generations, generational curses, generational demonization transfer.

(I will only give examples – more details are in my book Praying Doctors)

Exodus 20:5 – *Thou shall not bow down to them nor serve them. For I, the LORD your God, am a jealous God, visiting the iniquity of the fathers upon the children to the third and fourth generations of those who hate Me,*

Exodus 34:6 & 7 – *And the LORD passed before him and proclaimed, "The LORD, the LORD God, merciful and gracious, longsuffering, and abounding in goodness and truth, keeping mercy for thousands, forgiving iniquity and transgression and sin, by no means clearing the guilty,* visiting the iniquity of the fathers upon the children and the children's children to the third and the fourth generation."

Deuteronomy 27 & 28 – *Old Testament comprehensive chapters on blessings and curses.*

Isaiah 47 – *Curses on the occult.*

The occult: Divination, tarot cards, horoscopes, witchcraft, sorcery, psychics, mediums, shamanism, magic, spiritism, etc.

Other religions: Hinduism, Buddhism, Jehova's Witnesses, Mormons, Santeria Witchcraft.

The new age: Transpersonal psychologies, reincarnation, mantras, Reiki.

Secret societies: Freemasons, Rosacrucians

Any abuse: Physical, mental, emotional, sexual

Sexual immorality of any kind

Addictions

Abortions

Divorces

Illnesses: Mental, emotional, physical

Ungodliness, unbelief, ignorance

2) Word Curses

    Toward us

    Toward others

    Toward ourselves

3) Personal sin

All mentioned in 1 and 2 but there are subtler sins which are very common in the church i.e. fear, unforgiveness, resentment, bitterness, lack of faith etc, which are major entrance doors for the demonic and major blocks to healing.

4) Inner emotional traumas

These require inner healing or healing of the memories. A lot of this book is about this area, which is a prevalent cause of demonization and illnesses, i.e. abandonment, shame, neglect, loss, with reactions such as rebellion, lusts, bitterness etc.

There are many other doors i.e. ungodly beliefs, inner vows, ungodly soul ties, ignorance, unbelief, unforgiveness, accidents, illnesses, demonized places and objects, even at times religion without Jesus.

Rene Pelleya-Kouri, M.D.

There are different degrees, levels of demonic influence, oppression, infestation, affliction. In Mark 5 we see the Gadarene demoniac, who dwelled in the tombs, broke chains and shackles, could not be tamed, crying out and cutting himself with stones.

This seems to be a case of demonic possession. Remember what we are – spirit, soul and body, or the Temple of God with the Holy of Holiest, the holy place or inner courts and the outer courts.

Jesus cleansed inner courts, soul and body. The Holy of Holiest, or our spirit, in connection with the Holy Spirit after our new birth, is untouchable.

Deliverance proper

1. Always do a prayer of protection before the ministry and a cutting free prayer after the ministry. I recommend Francis MacNutt's Prayer of Protection. It is conveniently printed on a blue card, obtainable at www.christianhealingmin.org, or just create your own prayer. It is always very important to keep this in mind.

2. Check Relationships: With The Godhead, and with each other

Be sure everybody is born again (has accepted Jesus as Lord and Savior).

It is a good practice to share a confession of faith prayer, repenting and renouncing personal sin, generational sin, Satan, witchcraft, all evil involvement and contamination, curses.

Have the team pray for healing of hurts that includes a forgiveness prayer for any and all offenses.

The whole ministry team should be baptized in the Holy Spirit, walk in the Spirit and have activated gifts of the Spirit.

Meet regularly for prayer, teachings, activations and impartations.

Get to know each other very well.

3. Then bind Satan, the strong man, and every evil spirit, in the Name of Jesus. Learn the spirits as revealed by the Holy Spirit and from the recipient's complaint and history (See appendix for demonic groupings).

4. Be persistent in commanding the demons to come out. It is our practice to ask the prayer recipient to take a deep breath and exhale the evil spirits. Many may begin to cough them out. Thank you Lord.

It is a good practice to hold deliverance instruction and activation on a monthly basis. After studying the Word, ask the group to stand up and decree the following:

> I command out of me in the name of Jesus Christ every spirit of _____ (whatever the class was about and whatever we receive from the Holy Spirit)

> I command them to leave me now in the name of Jesus Christ.

> Everybody take a deep breath and let them out, cough them out, command them out unto the feet of Jesus, never to return. Go through these series of commands with different demonic groupings.

> Always infill with the Holy Spirit so the 'house' does not stay empty and let worse spirits come in.

> Keep your deliverance!

Our Experience Abroad

This training has been very effective. While ministering to 700 people in a church in Uganda in 2009, I was invited to do deliverance in 15 minutes! I did not want to do it but the Lord really pushed me. I commanded demons of generational curses that included witchcraft, occultism, sexual sin, abuse, demons of personal sin that included the above, abortions etc, and the demons of emotional traumas, unforgiveness, rejection, bitterness, rape etc. There was a *deliverance explosion*!

First of all the whole church came forward when I asked who wanted to be delivered, then as I commanded these spirits to come out there was massive deliverance, with every kind of manifestation. It was the Kingdom of God, Heaven invading the Earth.

We then called for an infilling of the Holy Spirit. Hundreds came to me and thronged me (I thought of Jesus) as I touched each person I just said, "Touch, Healing, Jesus, Freedom, etc and the people received more of God. Thank you Lord.

CHAPTER FIVE
"SIX STRONGHOLDS THAT OPPOSE LOVE AND HEALING"

Stronghold, a definition

– a fortified place occupied by strangers. Strongholds are empowered by the "occupation of strangers." These are places of wounding in our past where shame, bitterness, doubt, and unbelief have been fortified over time as we have not yielded ourselves to the truth of the gospel of Jesus Christ.

Stronghold, as demonstrated in Scripture

Jeremiah 51:51 – *We are ashamed because we have heard reproach. Shame has covered our faces, For strangers have come into the sanctuaries of the LORD's house.*

Jeremiah 51:53 – *Though Babylon were to mount up to heaven, And though she were to fortify the height of her strength, Yet from Me plunderers would come to her," says the LORD.*

HEALING, Our HERITAGE

The full Gospel of Jesus Christ includes healing. Jesus manifested the Love of God. Love without Healing is not the full Gospel. Love manifests Healing. Jesus healed all **who** came to Him. He did what He saw the Father doing (John 5:19,20.) Jesus, who is love, has compassion and healed all who came to Him. He commissioned us to heal and to do as He did. He gave us the Holy Spirit so we could fulfill that commission.

We cannot deny the gospel of healing. Jesus is the same, yesterday, today and forever. He gave us the Holy Spirit and the Kingdom of God so we would do the same things He did: Heal the sick and say to them "the Kingdom of God has come near to you".

Our Condition

Because we have lived in this fallen world, we have allowed the woundings in our history to become vulnerable to the "occupation" of the enemy. Without complete dependence upon the Holy Spirit, continued communion and intimacy with members in the Body of Christ, we allow unforgiveness, shame and bitterness to take up residence in us, and without our awareness, these strongholds are constantly being fortified by lies of the enemy. Many of us have believed the enemy's lies, as events in our lives seem to "affirm" his whispers to us. For example, if our parents divorced when we were young, and we 'believed' it was our fault, as is common with children, we continue to carry guilt and shame from broken relationship that does not belong to us. The wound of shame and false guilt are now open and we continue to be injured. A simple childhood argument results in our belief that we are unworthy of friendship, and on and on it goes, until the 'territory is fortified by strangers.' Pray and ask the Holy Spirit to illuminate areas in your life hidden by darkness, where wounds of rejection and bitterness, shame and guilt have been fortified by lies of the enemy. Now ask for His Truth to penetrate the darkness as you read the following Scriptures to yourself.

HIS REMEDY

Read the following scriptures aloud (faith comes by hearing the word of God):

Acts 1:8

Matt 10:1,7,8

Mark 16:15-20

John 14:12

Matt 4:23-25

Matt 28:16-20

Mark 6:55,56

Luke 4:40

Luke 6:17-19

Luke 9:1,2,6

Luke 10:9

Acts 5:16

OUR TESTIMONY

Release from the Stronghold of Deaf & Dumb Spirit

While ministering in Tanzania in 2010, a family brought me a young girl who was deaf from birth "That the doctors could not help". I laid hands on her ears and commanded the deaf-dumb spirit to leave her in the name of Jesus and declared total healing of her auditory system. She immediately heard and the crowd rejoiced.

When her family (of about ten people) entered, her mother shared that they were of the Muslim religion but wanted the Jesus that healed her daughter. They all accepted Jesus as Lord and Savior. Hallelujah! The power of God healed that child and the family was saved.

This is the Gospel of Jesus: The Gospel of salvation, healing, deliverance, signs and wonders, The Gospel of the Kingdom. Thank You, God

Love, like faith, is an action, is an activity. God is Love. The Nature of God is Love. Jehova Rapha: His love nature heals.

Jesus taught and preached the Gospel of The Kingdom of God and healed the sick. This is His pattern for us.

Love is the manifest presence of God that brings Healing. Love is the power of God in action. Love is Healing.

Just preaching about Love is not the same. It can become a religious kind of love, 'empty' as stated in I Cor 13: 1.

When the Love of God is present, it is active. Jesus came to manifest the love of God. It manifested in healing. That's what Jesus did. He loved and healed.

Six strongholds opposing love and healing:

Bitterness and Roots of Bitterness (Judgment and Unforgiveness) (Heb 12:14,15)

Unbelief (Heb 3:12,19)

Fear (Romans 14:23, 2 Tim 1:7)

Shame (Phil 3:19, Joel 2:26, Isaiah 61:7)

Rejection (Isaiah 53:3)

Control (1 Sam 15:23)

1. Bitterness and Roots of Bitterness: a definition

Bitterness and roots of bitterness are born of judgment due to real or perceived hurts or offenses. **Usually formed in childhood,** these 'judgments' are the response of our fallen nature in its attempts to protect from future pain. In reality, they are tools of the enemy that prevent us from the freedom of forgiveness, and our true identity in Christ.

Bitter Root Judgments, Demonstrated in Scripture

Heb 12:14-15 – *Make every effort to live in peace with everyone and to be holy; without holiness no one will see the Lord. See to it that no one falls short of the grace of God and that no bitter root grows up to cause trouble and defile many.*

Exodus 20:12 – *Honor your father and your mother, that your days may be long upon the land which the LORD your God is giving you.*

Romans 2:1 – *Therefore you are inexcusable, O man, whoever you are who judge, for in whatever you judge another you condemn yourself; for you who judge practice the same things.*

Matthew 7:1 – *"Judge not, that you be not judged."*

Matthew 18:35 – *"So My heavenly Father also will do to you if each of you, from his heart, does not forgive his brother his trespasses."*

Matthew 6:14-15 – *"For if you forgive men their trespasses, your heavenly Father will also forgive you. But if you do not forgive men their trespasses, neither will your Father forgive your trespasses.*

Mark 11:25 – *And whenever you stand praying, if you have anything against anyone, forgive him, that your Father in heaven may also forgive you your trespasses.*

Ask God today to give you the heart that forgives 70x7 (Luke 17:4).

Our Condition

Bitterness and roots of bitterness grow from the response of our sinful nature to people who have injured us. In this state, we either refuse to forgive or, more accurately, are unable to forgive. Our 'natural' response then, to offense is judgment, resentment, and bitterness

Most of the time, these bitter root judgments are formed in childhood against our parents and/or others who have been in authority over us. We can hold these judgments against people in our present or past, even someone who is already dead!

Keep in mind, it is these judgments, formed in childhood that can affect our current intimate relationships—even our relationship with Our Lord. It is our perception of their 'evil intent' towards us, our perception of seemingly harmless actions that lead us to this place of bitterness. We hold these as 'protection' from future pain, and they form a complex root system where all kinds of resentment, anger and even rage can grow, making it difficult, if not impossible to form trusting intimate relationships in adulthood.

An example might be of the youngest of three children born into a family of limited income. At meal time, it appears that everyone gets 'first' choice of the dinner offering, and they get 'last' or crumbs. The child sees this as an offense, and decides that parents and siblings have joined in the effort to belittle him. He then makes a 'judgment' against his family, and a pronouncement concerning his adult eating choices: "I will never take last again, and I will ALWAYS GET AS MUCH AS I WANT." You can see the work of the enemy, leading this person to addictive behaviors.

There are wounds that lead to bitterness. As previously stated, wounds inflicted upon us as children lead to bitterness. The following is a list of woundings that can lead to bitterness:

Every type of abuse: mental, physical, sexual,

Neglect,

Lack,

Rejection,

Abandonment

Humiliation…

Our reaction to these types of injuries is self protection. We become encased in a bitter shell. We create a heart of stone. There is no place for love in bitterness. There is no place for God in bitterness. Bitterness is a poison that blinds the eyes, deafens the ears, waxes the heart so we cannot get healed (Matt 13:14-15).

Bitterness operates as an octopus that takes over and grows. We become bitterness. Instead of the image of God we take on the image of the enemy. Conflict, strife, division, quarrels, envy, jealousy and depression characterize us.

There are seven spirits related to bitterness:

Spirit of unforgiveness

Spirit of resentment

Spirit of retaliation

Spirit of anger and wrath

Spirit of hatred

Spirit of violence and attack

Spirit of murder: Physical murder and suicide; Murder by the tongue (curses); Murder in the heart and separation.

His Remedy

*Prayer to be set free from bitterness:

Thank you Lord that when you became my Lord and Savior and I repented from all my sin and evil, I received the fullness of the atonement that includes all blessings from heavenly places in Christ.

I was saved, healed, delivered, FORGIVEN, redeemed, sanctified, set apart, made righteous. Thank you Lord!

Today, I lay the ax to the root of bitterness.

I repent and renounce unforgiveness, resentment, retaliation, anger and wrath, hatred, violence, attack, murder.

Thank you Lord, that your word says in 1 John 1:9 that if we confess our sins you are faithful to forgive us our sins and to cleanse us from all unrighteousness. Lord, I know that I have been offended by many. Today I forgive my parents, siblings, family members, friends, acquaintances, co-workers, teachers, ministers, husband, wife, children, and anyone that has hurt me, abused me, wounded me, betrayed me, rejected me, abandoned me, humiliated me, controlled me, intimidated me, dominated me. Lord, you forgave me, I forgive all and I forgive myself.

Thank you Jesus that I am under your blood. You took all my dysfunction into the cross. Thank you Lord that I have been set free, free indeed. I have your Life, the everlasting Life, the abundant Life.

The old has passed away, I am a new creation. The roots of bitterness have been utterly destroyed. I walk now in newness of life, in the liberty by which you have set me free.

Amen

2. Unbelief

Heb 3:12 – *Beware, brethren, lest there be in any of you an evil heart of unbelief in departing from the living God;*

Heb 3:19 – *So we see that they could not enter in because of unbelief.*

Isaiah 5:13,14 – *Therefore my people have gone into captivity, Because they have no knowledge; Their honorable men are famished, And their multitude dried up with thirst. Therefore Sheol has enlarged itself. And opened its mouth beyond measure; Their glory and their multitude and their pomp, And he who is jubilant, shall descend into it.*

Hosea 4:6,7 – *My people are destroyed for lack of knowledge. Because you have rejected knowledge, I also will reject you from being priest for Me; Because you have forgotten the law of your God, I also will forget your children. The more they increased, The more they sinned against Me; I will change their glory into shame.*

Our Condition

Unbelief implies living in the flesh. The flesh opposes the spirit and the spirit opposes the flesh. Unbelief is a substance of flesh and a substance of the world.

The cause of unbelief can be a **generational** curse, i.e. the Freemason's hoodwink. Unbelief is the worst poison as it can leads to eternal damnation. John 16:8, 9 - And when He has come, He will convict the world of sin, and of righteousness, and of judgment: of sin, because they **do not believe in Me; (emphasis, author's).**

One of the promises Jesus made was that the Holy Spirit would reprove the world of the sin of unbelief. Unbelief opposes The Healing of The Lord – He could not do great miracles in His home town because of unbelief (Matt 13:58).

In John's Gospel (John 12:37-40), *we see that there is a relationship between unbelief and a specific curse: Blind eyes, deaf ears, a waxed or hardened heart and an inability to be saved or healed.*

Jesus often confronted his apostles on their unbelief: Matt 16:5-12, Mark 9:14-29, John 20:27-29, Mark 16:14-20.

Christ promised believers that "these signs shall follow them that believe; In my name shall they cast out devils; they shall speak with new tongues;" (Mark 16:17-18)

If these signs are not being manifest in your life, it is possible that there is a ***stronghold***--a "home town", or "city", of unbelief inside. These territories, or strongholds of familiar spirits stop the flow of Love's healing power through us. They can quench our spirit.

Unbelief appeared at the Fall, and has increased steadily with the advancement of civilization. Following is a list of periods of such advancement in our society:

Age of reason, intellect, modern man

Age of enlightenment

Age of science

Age of rationality

Age of humanism

Age of philosophy

Age of religion

Greek mind

Descartes, a father of modern philosophy goes so far as to state: "I think, therefore I am", ascribing our *very existence to our thought process.*

Without the Lordship of Jesus Christ, these ideas are demonic implants, strongholds that oppose God, love, and healing. These positions oppose the Spirit.

The church exists in unbelief. Belief is in the heart. Belief is in the Spirit. The church has become spiritless. We **need** The Holy Spirit to convict us of the sin of unbelief.

The whole world is in sin. Civilization has been infected by Blind, deaf, and dumb spirits. We have been sequestered, kidnapped: exiled from miracles, signs and wonders, healing, and deliverance. We have been separated from the **Truth, and true faith in our Mighty God**.

We live as the world, preaching a gospel without the manifest power of God. Love is the power of God in action, doing good and healing everywhere (Act 10:38).

His Remedy

As we follow our Lord Jesus, transformed by His True Love, miracles of healing will manifest. He said "If you love me, you will obey me. You will do the things I do and more" (John 12:14). We pray for an intractable hunger for the presence of God. We cry out to Him to release all that implies *'us'* in the flesh: *our soul, personality, ideas, concepts, issues, emotions, feelings, things, the past:* **the old man.**

We depend upon Our Helper to bring about the complete death of our 'false self', so that the King can rule *in us*, and we can be **filled** with His presence, His faith, His glory, His gifts. We want the life of The Kingdom, the life of love and miracles to be manifest. We desire the *supernatural life* of God.

3. Fear

Our Condition

Fear is one of our worst enemies. The Apostle Paul (2 Tim 1:7) encourages us with this truth: God has not given us a spirit of fear, but of power and love and a sound mind. When we are fearful, we exhibit qualities that are the complete opposite of power, love and a sound mind. It is clear, then, that it is our enemy who would oppose the power of God, the love of God and the sound mind of Christ.

Fear BLOCKS the flow of supernatural ministry of God through us--miracles, signs and wonders Jesus promised as He commissioned us in Mark 16: 14-20.

There is a stronghold of fear of the generations. It is a familiar spirit that is hooked to our wounding and our shame. **Romans 8:15 says that we did not receive the spirit of bondage again to fear, but we received the spirit of adoption by whom we cry out Abba, Father.**

In Romans 14:23 we read that whatever is not from faith is sin.

Fear is related to image, our image of our *selves*, apart from God. Fear, then, is empowered by what we think, what we feel, who we are, as part of our *wrong identity*. Col 1:27 says that I have Christ in me, the hope of glory! No fear! I can do all things through Christ who strengthens me (Phil 4:13), but it seems that many still live in a **wrong flesh identity**. The old man: its concepts, ideas, emotions, ungodly beliefs. We can NOT do what Jesus said we would do as we continue to live in our flesh.

The best preaching, without power, without miracles, signs, wonders, healing and deliverance is dead preaching. This powerless preaching is but a vain imagination, the product of fear and unbelief.

In order to rid ourselves of fear we must undergo deliverance. We begin by deciding to enlist **God's plan** for our lives instead of our own!

His Remedy

We declare the truth of Galatians 2:20 – I have been crucified with Christ and **I no longer live**, but Christ lives in me. The life I now live in the body, I live by faith in the Son of God, who loved me and gave himself for me.

If we truly have the love of God in us, if we truly love, we live as Jesus lived: completely submitted to Our Father. We recognize that the old (man, our flesh) has gone and the new (man, alive to Jesus) has come. As we learn to walk in newness of life, we begin to operate by faith, free from fear! Faith without works is dead, love without works is dead. 1 John 4:18 – there is no fear in love, but perfect love casts out fear.

Read Psalm 27:1, Isaiah 35:4, Luke 12:32

Root out the generational stronghold of fear, lay the axe to the root, get it out. Repent and renounce it, circumcise your heart. Reclaim the territory given up by your ancestors. We are more than conquerors through Him who loved us (Romans 8:37).

Finally, engraft this commandment into your heart. Joshua 1:9 – "Have I not commanded you? **Be strong and courageous. Do not be afraid;** do not be discouraged, for the LORD your God will be with you *wherever you go*."

Amen

4. Shame

Our Condition

Shame is a painful emotion. It is experienced as a sense of guilt, embarrassment, unworthiness, disgrace, condemnation, dishonor, disappointment, deep-seated hurt, or felt as a *heaviness* in the heart.

Shame attacks us at the Core of our identity. We feel deformed, flawed, unlovable, unworthy, ugly, deficient, inferior. We experience a continuous fear of exposure, a feeling that something is 'wrong with me', or further, that *my very existence* is a mistake. Deep inside, there is a conviction that there is something wrong with us, something wrong *in* us. Shame says that we are defective, that we can't do, that we can't be who God says we are.

Shame is a <u>major weapon</u> of the devil. It has a powerful stranglehold on us. It brings us to destruction every time. Shame pushes us to sin. **Shame is at the core of addictions** because it is the unfillable hole, causing endless hunger. It is the place of condemnation.

Shame attempts to receive all it can from the flesh and the world. Shame *does not know God and opposes God.*

Shame splits us. Shame **wars** against <u>sonship</u>, <u>priesthood</u> and <u>kingship</u>. It opposes our inheritance, it says "How can you be an heir?"

As stated in Philippians 3:18-20, "Many live as enemies of the cross of Christ. Their destiny is destruction, their god is their stomach, and their glory is in their shame. Their mind is set on earthly things. But *our* citizenship is in heaven."

It is clear. We *must* get rid of shame!

His Remedy

God has healed all our wounds on the cross. Appropriate the total healing of the cross – shame can't bind us anymore. We are the people of God and <u>we have been made whole</u>. Shame be gone in the name of Jesus. Receive your double portion.

Joel 2:26 – My people shall never be put to shame.

Isaiah 61:7 – Instead of your shame you shall have double honor.

5. Rejection (He is despised and rejected Isaiah 53:3)

Rejection is a main wound. We can carry a spirit of rejection that opposes the Love of God. We live a life of rejection, even expecting to be rejected. There are spirits of rejection inside of us, seeking rejection. We must again forgive our parents for rejecting us, neglecting us, not honoring us, not nurturing us, not embracing us, not holding us, not encouraging us, not supporting us, not protecting us, not giving us warmth, not blessing us, not saying "I love you", not releasing the love of God into us, controlling us.

Today we **hold onto** Abba. Our Lord took our rejection into His body on the cross. He said "Father why hast thou abandoned me?"

Abandonment: The Worst Pain Possible!

Of all the wounds inflicted upon us as children, abandonment, rejection, and separation cause the deepest pain. The Lord is rescuing you today. He is filling you up with Himself. His fullness, His love, His identity. You are in His image – receive.

6. Spirit of Control

Can be acquired in the womb. Generational spirit of control for survival. Deeply embedded survival generational spirits of control since the fall. It is a rebellious power-seeking spirit: Control, domination, intimidation.

It is a spirit of death that destroys relationships and families. It is a spirit of division. It totally opposes love. It is an occultic sexual spirit by the name of <u>sexual witchcraft</u>. It is temple prostitution. It includes abortion, incest, fornication, adultery, pornography, homosexuality. It is a perverse spirit. It is the hallmark of iniquity. It is a religious spirit. It is a major antichrist spirit. It is the dragon that has fallen into the earth. It is Jezebel and its offspring. It is an angry spirit. It brings accusation, condemnation, attack. It judges. It is totally contrary to love. It wants to dominate, abuse and squash its victims. It is a bipolar mood disorder spirit. It is a borderline demon. <u>It is doubleminded</u>. It is an addiction demon. It requires major inner healing and major deliverance. <u>It is born out of wounds</u>. It is a defensive-aggressive spirit that has taken over the personality. It is a self-righteous demon that has been assigned to 'protect' the wounded self. We have to peel layer after layer.

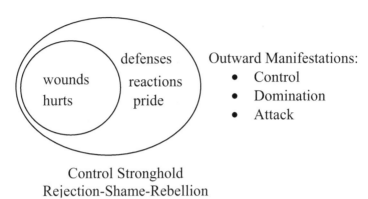

Control Stronghold
Rejection-Shame-Rebellion

The whole system has to be eradicated. It has in itself the previous 5 strongholds (bitterness, unbelief, fear, shame, rejection).

Only God can do this. No therapy, guidance or religion will get rid of this evil. It can be defeated in the one step program, like in the case of Paul, or it might require the 12 step program – a process. Anyway, the Christian life is a progressive conquering of inner and outer lands.

Prayer To Destroy The Six Strongholds

In the name of Jesus Christ and by the power of His cross and His blood, we repent and renounce every sinful word, every judgment, accusation, and condemnation that has come out of our mouths and of the mouths of our generations:

Sinful words against God

Against our parents

Against ministers

Against our spouses, children

Against anybody else

Against ourselves

In the name of Jesus Christ, break and cancel the power of all word curses in our lives and in our families. In the name of Jesus Christ and by the power of His blood and His cross we confess, repent and renounce:

<u>Defeat and discouragement</u> and the principality of defeat and discouragement

<u>Bitterness</u> and the principality of bitterness

<u>Unbelief</u> and the principality of unbelief

<u>Fear</u> and the principality of fear

<u>Shame</u> and the principality of shame

<u>Rejection</u> and the principality of rejection

<u>Control</u> and the principality of control

We accept, have revelation of Jesus' atonement on the cross and receive forgiveness, healing, deliverance and all provisions. We receive the full inheritance in Jesus Christ by the promise of the spirit.

Deliverance Proper *(see chapter 4 on deliverance)*

We will command demons out from the discussed areas.

1. Stronghold of bitterness

In the name of Jesus Christ I command spirits of bitterness and all related spirits to come out of me. Bitterness, roots of bitterness, unforgiveness, resentment, retaliation, anger, hatred, violence, frustration, revenge, judgement, accusation, condemnation, rebellion, strife

I command them to leave me now

Take a deep breath and let them all out. Cough them out. Keep naming them. Cleanse the house, send them to the feet of Jesus, never to return. At the end we will infill ourselves with the Holy Spirit and Godliness.

2. Stronghold of unbelief

    A) In the name of Jesus Christ I command all spirits of unbelief to come out of me, cessationistic religious spirits, freemasons hoodwink, other religious cults and the occult spirits, new age spirits, spiritual psychologies spirits, blind eyes, deaf ears, waxed heart spirits, deaf dumb spirits, every demonic implant in our spirits, minds, emotions, soul, spirits that have infected modern civilization, vain imagination spirits, spirits of dead works, humanism, philosophy, intellectualism.

    B) I command them all to leave me now.

    C) Take a deep breath and let them all out. Cough them out. Keep commanding them to leave you in the name of Jesus Christ. Send them to the feet of Jesus, never to return.

3. Stronghold of fear

    A) In the name of Jesus Christ I command spirits of fear to come out of me. Wrong identity, false self, familiar spirits, vain imaginations, faith without works, generational fear, fear in the womb, bondage to fear.

B) I command them all to leave me now.

C) Take a deep breath and let them all out. Cough them out. Keep commanding them to leave you in the name of Jesus Christ. Send them to the feet of Jesus, never to return.

4. Stronghold of shame

A) In the name of Jesus Christ I command out of me all spirits of shame, wrong identity, hunger and lust, addiction, guilt, condemnation, iniquity, unworthiness, unlovable, deformed, deficient, inferior.

B) I command them all to leave me now.

C) Take a deep breath and let them all out. Cough them out. Keep commanding them to leave you in the name of Jesus Christ. Send them to the feet of Jesus, never to return.

5. Stronghold of rejection

A) In the name of Jesus Christ I command out of me all evil spirits of rejection, neglect, abandonment, separation, lack, loneliness, isolation, wounds, hurts.

B) I command them all to leave me now

C) Take a deep breath and let them all out. Command them out. Name and cough them out. Send them to the feet of Jesus. Command them not to return.

6. Stronghold of Control

A) In the name of Jesus Christ I command out of me all spirits of control, witchcraft, condemnation, accusation, intimidation, domination, pride, attack, blame, antichrist, jezebel, dragon, double minded, religious spirits, perverse spirits, sexual witchcraft, incest, fornication, temple prostitution, abortion, death.

B) I command them all to leave me now

C) Take a deep breath and let them all out. Command them out, never to return. Send them to the feet of Jesus. Command them not to return.

We will also pray against the strongholds of defeat and discouragement, very prevalent here and in third world countries.

7. Strongholds of defeat and discouragement

A) In the name of Jesus Christ I command out of me Jebusite spirits of defeat and discouragement, downtrodden, grasshopper, defeat, failure, tired, hope deferred, unworthiness, worthlessness, self-pity, depression.

B) I command them all to leave me now

C) Take a deep breath and let them out. Cough them out. Command them not to return. Send them to the feet of Jesus.

Post Deliverance

We need to infill our house with the Holy Spirit. We call upon the Holy Spirit to fill up every part of us. We ask God to release mantles and anointing= love and healing.

Peace Shalom and sweetness instead of bitterness

Supernatural faith and love instead of unbelief

Holy boldness and strength instead of fear (Luke 12:32, 1 John 4:8, 2 Timothy 1:7)

Honor, holiness, righteousness instead of shame

Acceptance in the Beloved instead of rejection

Submission, yielding and surrendering to the Holy Spirit and the will of God instead of control, rebellion and stubbornness

Victory in Christ instead of defeat, failure, and discouragement

Divine healing instead of sickness, disease and infirmity of spirit, soul and body

I assure you that at the end of this deliverance you will have much less of the demonic load. You will be freer and will start at a higher place of the Victory of the Cross, and not only that, but you will have learned self-deliverance. You can implement these principles of deliverance at any time.

We need to develop discernment, and as we assess that some evil spirits have attached to us we command them out and abide in the freedom that is in Christ.

We thank, praise and worship our God for our total salvation (sozo) of spirit, soul and body.

We thank you Father, Son and Holy Spirit.

Amen.

CHAPTER SIX
"THE CHILD"

In this Chapter we investigate the many characteristics of our wounded inner child. Invite the Holy Spirit to direct you to the one that resonates inside and allow its healing.

The entrance door of the generational curses establishes the wounding of the child.

I need you Lord, Let me speak your word in your power; In the power of the Holy Spirit, not away from you, but by abiding in you. Without you I can do nothing. My vine, My king, My Lord and my God, through you I overcome all fears that are now receding. The unconquerable cross. Life emanates from your cross. Messiah you came; little children worship you. Satan's focus is to hurt and kill children, little heirs, little kings, little sons, are murdered everywhere.

Inner children are hurt and devastated, kept in prisons. Wounded, hurt, abused, rejected, abandoned, humiliated, controlled, squashed, neglected. The family's agenda falls on the child. Generational curses of child sacrifice pursue the child = the loss of the child. Massive forces overwhelm him and imprison him. Man needs to survive. Survival mechanisms arise that further bury the child. We have buried children inside.

"The voice of your brother's blood is crying to Me from the ground"

Little children are the sheep of Your green pasture. You came to save the lost. We all have someone lost inside of us. Our greatest loss: generations of lost children cry from the ground.

There was the exchange of the cross. The child Jesus (The Son of the Father) died so that my hidden child could have life.

He came to heal the brokenhearted, set the captives free, open prison doors, heal the sick, resurrect the dead.

There is an attack on the child, the attack against the exchange. Enemies of the cross side with the world. (Phil 3.19)

The major attack is against the child. The major wound is in the child.

We reject our wound,

We reject the child,

We deny and repress,

Put away,

Place in captivity,

"We must live"

We learn a pattern

A pattern of putting away

(Pharaoh, Herod, Ataliah, Molech, Ammon, Amnon, Abbadon, Jezabel-Ahab, Leviathan etc.)

Every new hurt goes to cover the child, to bury him deeper and deeper. <u>We do have self-hate.</u> We are unable to follow the commandments of our Lord – love yourself, love your neighbor. If we don't love ourselves or our neighbor we can't fully love God. <u>We live in sin</u> = permanent open doors. <u>The sin of self-hate, self-rejection.</u> Layer upon layer we bury our hurts.

We end up not being honest.

<u>Salvation lies inside.</u>

<u>We believe with the heart</u> but our hearts are imprisoned.

Lord touch our hearts.

We exalt ourselves.

We bury our child.

Sins of the fathers = sacrifice of the child.

Generational pattern of child sacrifice.

Self-centeredness abandons the child.

God-centeredness resurrects the child.

(Jeremiah 31: 15, 16, 17 hope at the end)

V15 Thus says the Lord,

"A voice was heard in Ramah,

Lamentation and bitter weeping,

Rachael weeping for her children,

Refusing to be comforted for her children, Because they are no more."

V16 Thus says the Lord,

"Refrain your voice from weeping,

And your eyes from tears;

For your work shall be rewarded, says the Lord.

And they shall come back from the land of the enemy.

There is hope in your future, says the Lord,

That your children shall come back to their own border."

The children hold onto the cross while the onslaught goes on outside.

They have escaped.

They are in exile.

Who is the greatest in the Kingdom? The Child.

Matthew: 18 – and He called a little child unto himself and put him in the midst of them

He rescued the child.

He accepted the child.

He took the child out of captivity.

He healed the child.

He washed the child clean.

He poured His blood upon the child.

He loved the child.

He honored the child.

He is proud of the child.

He put him in the midst of them.

V3 He said repent.

Become like the child.

Let the child out.

Let the child teach you.

Innocent.

Vulnerable.

Pure.

Trusting.

Loving.

Lowly.

Forgiving.

V4 Humble yourselves.

Matthew 18:4-5 *Therefore whoever humbles himself as this little child is the greatest in the kingdom of heaven. Whoever receives one little child like this in My name receives Me.*

Out of captivity.

To receive Jesus.

Need to receive, accept, welcome the little child.

There is a War for the child.

Strongholds of captivity.

Fortresses with the hidden child inside.

Every evil thing mounted up against the child.

Introjections from family.

Spirit of introjections – identification.

Transference – projection.

V10 – Take heed that you do not despise one of these little ones, for I say to you that in heaven their angels always see the face of My Father who is in heaven.

VS 11-For the Son of Man has come to save that which was lost.

The child is hidden with Christ.

Receive the child.

Receive Christ.

Come Holy Spirit.

Look into my heart.

Look into the heart of the child.

Heal the broken heart.

Open prison doors.

Set the captives free.

[Isaiah 61] Appropriate the exchange of the cross.

Give them beauty instead of ashes

Oil of joy instead of mourning

Garment of praise for spirit of heaviness

Oaks of righteousness

Planting of the Lord

Glorify Him

There is an exchange of strongholds.

Jeremiah 31:28b - I will watch over them to build and to plant.

Rebuild ancient ruins

Raise up former desolations

Renew the ruined cities

Devastation of many generations

Of murdering the child

Of sacrificing the child

Living lives of lies

Rene Pelleya-Kouri, M.D.

Facades

Masks

Society

The world

Sinful lives

A) We do repent / confess / renounce

B) We receive the exchange

The Lord has opened prison doors and he has let my child free. There is life inside, life in my heart. I have a new heart and a new spirit. The free child is in my heart. The true self is alive.

He inherits the kingdom

I can now receive Christ in my heart

I can now abide in Christ

I am not split

I have no hidden agendas

I am called the priest of the Lord

The minister of my God

Instead of our former shame

We have a double recompense

Everlasting joy

Everlasting covenant

And our offspring, our children that have been set free shall be known among the nations. They will be recognized as true people that the Lord has blessed. I will greatly rejoice in the Lord. He has clothed me with the garments of salvation. He has covered me with the robe of righteousness. As a bride, he has adorned me with jewels. The Lord will cause righteousness and praise to spring forth before all the nations. Hallelujah. (Isaiah 61)

My wife Betty and I married while being fully in Christ. She as well as myself had devastating previous relationships. After I was filled with the Holy Spirit, I lived in total celibacy for several years. This is definitely one of the biggest miracles that I have seen in my life. Since the age of 13 years old, when I had sex with a prostitute, I had been obsessed with sex. I never learned about love. Betty and I were obedient to our God, we had no sexual involvement until we got married. After our marriage we were full of joy and serving our Lord, still hidden issues never dealt with popped up when we engaged in progressive intimacy. We had issues that war against each other. On my side there was my mother's intrusion and the reactions to intrusion. On Betty's side there was her father's intrusion and the reactions to intrusion.

Abuse

Abandonment

Rejection

Betrayal

Shame

Child sacrifice

Defenses and reactions

Rebellion

Lusts

Witchcraft

Control

Addiction

Codependency

Accusation

Condemnation

Doing the same thing that was done to us.

Demonization

Jezebel wants to destroy ministries. She is born out of deep abuse. Rejection, worthlessness, shame. She is out to avenge herself, to control and dominate and eventually to destroy. I am a Son of the King that is under attack. I fall in the trap and react. Intrusion has been a weak link in my life. Intrusion is at the door and underneath the wound. Of course I have forgiven my mother and love her with my heart, but it was beyond my mother. My grandfather was a great 33 free mason, general inspector, famous physician and professor. He had major issues of anger, control and domination. Rebellion rises up against intrusion. It becomes witchcraft versus witchcraft. Sprits of witchcraft fighting against each other. The stronghold of bitterness rises up against intrusion, disrespect, and humiliation. There is hidden rejection, abandonment and shame;

unforgiveness, resentment, retaliation, anger, wrath, hatred, violence, murder. Intrusion is the spirit of murder.

Molech, Leviticus 18:21, Leviticus 20:1-5 (Child sacrifice)

We need to get rid of the spirit of intrusion.

Cain, Pharoah, Herod

Matthew 2:18

Ataliah killed the royal seed, but the Son of the King was protected.

Matthew 18:3 The child enters the Kingdom of God.

The Lord has protected the little king inside of us.

The Holy child, the Son of God died on the cross so our child and our children will have life.

Lord, I want you to rule in my emotional life with my wife.

There is a whirlwind of emotions, moods, feelings and affects.

The emotions of the personality

A personality of emotions

An area out of control

Not under rational control

Self-willed emotions

Complexes

Underneath things that act out

Rene Pelleya-Kouri, M.D.

The emotions of humankind

Generational emotions

Generational curses over the emotions

Emotional demonization

Infestation

Demonic influences on the emotions

Hidden emotions

Emotional unfinished business

Reactive emotions

Emotions of defense

Emotions of attack

Pockets of infestations

Emotional attacks

The emotions of the flesh

The face of emotions

Anger, attack

Hurt, hidden, repressed

I have fear and I am feared

Anger as defense

Retaliation

Revenge

<u>Characteristics of the hidden child. The hidden personality with afflicted emotions that keeps acting out.</u>

A crying child, an unheard child, an abandoned child, a rejected child, a humiliated child, an abused child, a neglected child, a discounted child, a dishonored child, an un-respected child, an unloved child, an unworthy child, a forgotten child, a squashed child, a lost child, a hidden child, an angry child, a rebellious child, a revengeful child, a bitter child, a defensive child, An attacking child, a controlling child, a quiet child, a silent child, a screaming child, a sacrificed child, a murdered child, a fantasy child, a seeking child, a demanding child, a never satisfied child, an accusing child, a condemning child, an addicted child, a codependent child, a protected child, an armored child, a lustful child, a defeated child, a self-pitying child, a self-hating child, an unrepentant child, an unforgiving child, a resentful child, a violent child, a wrathful child, an imprisoned child, a stubborn child, a timid child, a fearful child, a weak child, an inferior child, a self-absorbed child, a self-centered child, the acting out child, the sacrificed child, the unnoticed child, the beaten child, the captive child, the imprisoned child, the brokenhearted child, the independent child, the lonely child, the fantasy child, the traumatized child, the lost rebellious child, the surviving child, the exiled child, the isolated child, the child king, the hostile child, the self-protected child, and the stubborn child.

Evil spirits can infect the wounded child and create an inner demonized stronghold.

(Hebrews 4:12)

Have to discern

Have to uncover

Have to bring light into hidden places

Have to expose every creature

A formed personality

The hidden emotional infected personality that acts out the familiar spirit of the hidden wounded child that acts out

Holy Spirit help me to discern

The world of the hidden child

The city of the hidden child

The kingdom of the child

The characteristics of the hidden child

The emotional life of the child

The stronghold of the child

A separate realm

A different universe

Generation after generation the child has to hide

The hidden child with its own life inside.

It does not want to conform to "adult reality", the abusive reality. It knows about the falseness and the dishonesty of the adult. Jesus came to bring peace, a special peace, not as the world knows it. He came to implement His Kingdom. He came to destroy the kingdom of darkness. He came to set the captives free, to open prison doors, to heal broken hearts, <u>to save the lost.</u>

Somehow he has to submit his kingdom to the Kingdom of God.

"I am on my own"

"I love my independence"

"I will never submit"

"I have to survive"

"You want to destroy me"

I hate you. You abandoned, neglected, humiliated, hurt me. You disregarded me, dishonored me, rejected me, forgot me.

The kingdom of the adult vs. the kingdom of the child

The world, surface life vs. inner life of the child

The emotions!

The child keeps acting out

Volcanoes erupt

Pandora's box opens up

The emotions of the child invade our consciousness, at times take over

There is a demonic infestation of the hidden world of the child

Devastations of many generations

Ruined cities inside

Old waste

Former desolation

Waste cities

We are the repairer of the breach

The restorer of the paths to dwell in

Isaiah 58: 6-12

Isaiah 61: 4

The kingdom of the lost child

"No one will take my life away from me"

Basically a rejection, neglect, abuse – rebellion, stubborn, angry stronghold

"I will defend this place unto death"

A city underneath

A life of its own

It is part of me

I carry it

It is a yoke

Do not keep attacking this hidden place

A life of strife is unsuccessful

All of me needs to be Holy – set apart

God loves unity – wholeness

A divided house falls

A spirit out of control has broken down walls

Double mindedness is a problem

God wants to take the whole land

Foreigners have invaded inner sanctuaries

The inner sanctuary of the child

The child made alliances with the enemy

Pacts and covenants

It had to survive

Time to end the strife

Both sides want peace

We will decontaminate the emotions

A washing by the water of the Word

All who call on the name of the Lord will be saved

The hidden emotions cry out

The core is <u>deep hurt</u> and <u>a need</u> to be recognized, accepted, loved

We repent of false alliances

We repent of every evil thing

Anger, power, control, rebellion, stubbornness, witchcraft, fear, bitterness, self-will, self-hate, self-rejection, hate, condemnation, attack

We repent of war and strife

Today we end the war

Today we end the generational war

Today we end the rule of Molech

Today we take over with <u>Jehovah Nissi</u> every hidden place

Today we recue the captured child

Today we honor that little child

Today we pour the love of God inside of ourselves through the Holy Spirit

Today is reconciliation, integration, wholeness

There is a new city

Peace, love, joy, righteousness, unity

I am one house under one King

We bow, submit, surrender, yield

Seek first the Kingdom of God and all will be added

I am the repairer of the breach

The restorer of the paths to dwell in

We have built over the old waste places and have raised up the former desolations – the desolations of many generations

I am a priest of the Lord and a minister of God

We have double portion and everlasting joy

We have an everlasting covenant

We are the seed that the land has blessed

Our children are blessed

Our child is blessed

Isaiah 62:12 – And they shall call them The Holy People, The Redeemed of the LORD; And you shall be called Sought Out, A City Not Forsaken.

Matthew 18:3 – the child of the kingdom of God

Emotions submitted to the King

Love never fails

The anointing breaks the yoke and opens prison doors

Let the kingdom come

Let the king rule

Let love rule

The old world has cracked

The old order is gone

There is a new order

The Kingdom of God

The sun of righteousness has come out

And there is healing in its wings

We have a king

We are united under one king

A mantle of the kingdom

A son, an heir

I submit to your rulership Lord

I have a new spirit

I have a new heart

I have a God

All of me is for you

Spirit, soul and body

Peace is within

Oil of gladness

Joy

Beauty

Praise

Righteousness

I want to glorify you God

Amen. Jesus!

A. Parents Prayer of Reconciliation-

Parents: We are sorry because we hurt you. When you were born, we rejoiced, you were an adorable shinning jewel. We had many wrong issues; unhealed places in us. We mistreated you, forgive us, we didn't recognize, accept, honor you, we rejected abandoned and betrayed you. We hurt you in spirit, soul and body. Forgive us, we look at you now and we again see that jewel, who you are, but shining even brighter. We are proud of you. We respect and honor you, we really love you, we embrace you.

B. Children's Prayer of Reconciliation-

Child: I was so hurt, felt so rejected and abandoned and full of shame, rebellion, bitterness. Unforgiveness and rage rose in me, I judged, blamed, accused and condemned you and at times I hated you. Today, the Lord Jesus has touched my heart. He had to break me and soften my heart.

Today I understand, how wounded you were! Jesus forgave me, I forgive you, I repent of judgment, unforgiveness, bitterness, rage, accusation, blame. Would you forgive me for my reactions towards you? God has poured Love into my heart by the Holy Spirit. I have new eyes and a new heart. I can honestly say that I love you today. I fully embrace you today.

Thank you Jesus!

Isaiah 61:6-11

CHAPTER SEVEN
"THE VOLCANO"

<u>So many years with a deep-seated and lingering disorder,</u> waiting for the bubbling up of the water (John 5). Yes I am thirsty Lord, I am supremely thirsty. All is chaos and destruction around me. Hell encamps very near me. I am into the pit. Bellies of whales encompass me. I am running away from you. I am running away from myself. I lay in miry clay. The enemy surrounds me and there is no way out for me.

So many years with a deep-seated and lingering disorder. It is me. I have not learned how to love me. Frailty. But a passing breath, dust and ashes will I be, no more to even think of You. But, I believe in Jesus, the Son gives life, I do as He did, I give life. My ears are open to His words. I listen to His message. I believe and trust. I cling and rely on Him who sent Jesus. <u>I posses now Eternal Life.</u> I don't come into judgment or condemnation. I have already passed over, out of death, <u>into life</u>. I have the boldness of free access to God (Ephesians 3).

There is a rich treasury of His glory. I am strengthened and reinforced with mighty power in the inner man. By the Holy <u>Spirit himself</u> that indwells my innermost being <u>and personality</u>. I have the power and strength to apprehend and grasp <u>the</u>

experience of the love of Christ. I have become a body wholly fulfilled and flooded with God Himself. Lord, only speak the word and I will be healed. Jesus says: "It shall be done for you as you have believed".

New levels of being in Christ

He works with the clay, reshuffling, changing and transforming, moving into truth. Mysteries being exposed, the Word of God opening up a deeper revelation of Christ, a deeper revelation of who I am in Christ. Invasion of experiential knowledge, which is the deeper knowledge needed to know God.

What part of me submerges in a pit with crocodiles?

Fallen humankind full of unbearable needs.

I want to be pleased

A burden of needing to please

A craving for control, domination, possession

An insatiable need

A fully instinctual being

The hunger

The wolf

Instincts out of control

The flesh

An infestation in the flesh

The infestation of the flesh

A sinful flesh

A flesh that wants to be pleased

The needs of the flesh

The needs of sinful flesh (flesh without God)

Hunger, craving, wants, desires, needs, longings

An unfillable hole

I want them all

Fantasies of control

Relentless lust

Cravings, perversions, iniquity, witchcraft

Sexual witchcraft

Temple prostitution

Ashtaroth poles

Lingams

Yonis

Idolatry

Abuse

Incest

Rape

Laws

A) The laws of the spirit of life in Christ Jesus.

The law of our new being (Romans 8)

Those who are in Christ Jesus and who live and walk after the dictates of the Spirit.

B) The law of sin and death

Those who walk after the dictates of the flesh

The Messiah yielded Himself to atone for our sins to save and sanctify us in order to rescue and deliver us from this present wicked age and world order. (Galatians 1 AMP)

Do not turn renegade and desert Him. Do not transfer your allegiance. The Messiah Himself revealed to Paul the true Gospel. God chooses us and sets us apart to reveal His Son within us.

Galatians 2:20 – I have been crucified with Christ; it is no longer I, who live, but Christ lives in me; and the *life* which I now live in the flesh, I live by faith in the Son of God, who loved me and gave Himself for me.

A life of Faith!

I live by faith and by adherence and reliance on, and complete trust and dependence on the Son of God who loved me and gave Himself up for me.

Now faith has come, I have been baptized into Christ and I have clothed myself with Christ. He purchased my freedom. I am adopted, I have sonship, I have the Holy Spirit of Jesus in my heart. I cry Abba Father. I am a son, I am an heir of God through Christ. Christ is being completely and permanently molded within me. <u>We who are born again</u> are not children of a slave woman. We are not <u>children of the flesh</u>. We are not children destined for slavery. We are not children in bondage. We are the children of the promise, we are the children of the Kingdom. We are the children of freedom (Galatians 4 AMP). In this freedom Christ has made us free and completely liberated us (Galatians 5 AMP). <u>Stand fast</u> and do not be hampered and held snared, and submit again to a yoke of slavery. Walk and live in the Holy Spirit, then you will not gratify the cravings and desires of <u>the flesh</u> (human nature without God). The desires of the flesh are opposed to the Holy Spirit, and the <u>desires of the spirit</u> are opposed to the flesh (godless human nature). These are antagonistic to each other, continually in conflict with each other.

Practices of the flesh:

Immorality, Adultery, Impurity, Fornication, Indecency, Uncleanness, Lasciviousness, Idolatry, Sorcery, Witchcraft, Hatred, Enmity, Variance, Strife, Jealousy, Wrath, Anger, Ill temper, Seditions, Selfishness, Divisions, Dissensions, Heresies, Party spirits, Factions, Sects, Peculiar opinions, Envy, Drunkenness, Carousing, Reveling, Covetousness

Those who belong to Christ have crucified the flesh (the godless human nature) with its passions, appetites and desires. If we live by the Holy Spirit let us also walk by the Holy Spirit. Let's walk in the spirit, have our life in God. Let us go forward walking in line, our conduct controlled by the Spirit.

For whatever a man sows, that and only that, is what he will reap, for he who sows to his own flesh (lower nature sensuality) will from the flesh reap <u>decay, ruin, destruction, corruption and disease</u>. But he who sows to the Spirit will from the Spirit reap

<u>eternal, everlasting life</u> (health). Be mindful to be a blessing (Galatians 6 AMP).

[See Romans 6,7,8]

A hunger, an insatiable hunger, that came because of lack of love. God is love. Love is the substance of life. Without love we perish. We didn't have God, we didn't have love, we perished. Consumed by flesh – sinful human nature without God, seeking love, seeking God. The enemy deceived all mankind, blinded groping in darkness, attempting to gain love through sinful flesh. Repetition compulsion in hell. The flesh is addicted to sex, it can never have enough. It can never find love – an endless search for love. We have been deceived, we have been lied to. We had a wrong father, we were of the other kingdom. We had allegiances to darkness. We were convinced that we could find love in the flesh. We were sowing into darkness, we reaped corruption, sickness and death.

Flesh begets flesh

Spirit begets spirit

We became children of the flesh, children of the curse, children of darkness

I want more

I need more

I have to treat my wounds

My pain is unbearable

I cover myself with poison to relieve my pain

Worse pain arises

Rene Pelleya-Kouri, M.D.

Darkness overwhelms me

I am in the pit

I have reached bottom

I have become a bottom feeder

I have become addicted to the excrements of hell

It tastes good to me

Layer after layer

Façade after façade

Mask after mask

A life of lies

I have mostly hidden my pain under tons of rubble

Devastations of the generations

Generations of children sacrificed

Life in the flesh

Life in the world

Blind

Deaf

Heart waxed

I cannot be saved or healed

The reality of God is absolutely hidden from me

I live a life of captivity

In the flesh

Into the flesh

Overwhelmed by the flesh

A life of covetousness

Covetousness as idolatry

Witchcraft, rebellion, stubbornness

Totally doomed

Covered by sadness

Living in darkness

Totally corrupt

Thinking that I am fine

Deceived to the end

But He came

He came to destroy the works of darkness

He forgave us

He took the curse away

He disarmed principality and powers

Rene Pelleya-Kouri, M.D.

He sent the word

God sent the word

The word is in the air

Today hear

He is calling

The Son came to save the world. He is opening roads in intractable barren lands, overwhelmed by hell. Layer after layer falls, cover-ups are exposed. His hand reaches to the core of the pain. There is a cry of hidden hearts:

I have never been loved

I don't know love

I am gasping for last breaths

I really want to die

I am hopeless

There is no help

I am covered by deadly darkness

The spirit of death is upon me

I have hurt so many

I keep stabbing myself

I hate myself

I am full of shame

I am beyond forgiveness

But He came

God so loved the world that He sent His only son to die for you. He endured the cross for the latter joy. You are His joy, you are His love. Prodigals come out of miry clay pits, come out of pig pens. Today call upon the name of the Lord, cry to Jesus. The word is in the air, hear the word of salvation.

He came for you. He came to save you. He came to deliver you from darkness. He came to heal your broken heart. He is healing you right now. Betrayal, shame, addictions, unforgiveness, hurt, rejection are leaving. God is spreading the love of Christ into your hearts through the Holy Spirit. Receive salvation, healing, deliverance. Receive the love of God in your hearts.

My God and my Lord

Only you Jesus

Only you

He heals your deepest hurt and He pours His love upon you

The healing love of Jesus

The Kingdom of God is at hand. The power of God that manifests signs, wonders, healing and miracles, deliverances, provision, reconciliation. The power of God is the Holy Spirit. God in me, the King. The Spirit of Jesus, the Holy Spirit, the ruler of the Kingdom. He manifests the Kingdom, he rules over the ministering angels. The Holy Spirit makes us who we are in Christ.

The atmosphere

The environment

The radius

The area

The place of the influence

The place where it manifests

A king

A kingdom

Citizens of the kingdom

Visible and invisible

Ambassador of the kingdom

Passport of the kingdom

Power

Authority

Gifts

Fruits

Jesus' Ministry

A commission to proclaim the good news of salvation

A commission to cast out devils

A commission to heal the broken hearts

A commission to open prison doors

A commission to set the captives free

A commission to heal those oppressed by the devil

We are going to begin to expose the whole panorama of the deep wounding and our reactions and defenses.

The Volcano

***volcano (d)**an opening in the earth's crust from which molten lava, rock fragments, ashes, dust, and gases are ejected from below the earth's surface*

Note: Volcanoes tend to occur along the edges of tectonic plates.

Note : Eruptions and lava flows associated with them can be very destructive. (See Mount Saint Helens and Mount Vesuvius.)

This picture and definition of an occurrence in our natural world can give us clarity as we prepare to minister to those who have been held captive to the strongholds associated with woundings of childhood.

As we view the diagram on page 89 with its 3 levels apparent to the eye, note the presentation, with smoke at the top representing 'presenting symptoms'. Secondly, level B the mountain of defenses, and lastly, not visible to the naked eye, the core where the hidden wounds reside.

---

*   Institute of Electrical and Electronics Engineers (IEEE): Dictionary. com, "volcano," in The American Heritage® Science Dictionary. Source location: Houghton Mifflin Company. http://dictionary. reference.com/browse/volcano. Available: http://dictionary.reference. com. Accessed: March 10, 2013.

We will use this volcano as a panorama of wounded man with different levels, layers or walls to help us minister healing and deliverance.

A) The core

B) Reactions and defenses

C) Surface smoke

We are going to expose the whole panorama of deep wounding along with our reactions and defenses, and present them to the powerful Light of the Truth, bringing God's healing love to the deepest places of rejection and hurt.

THE VOLCANO

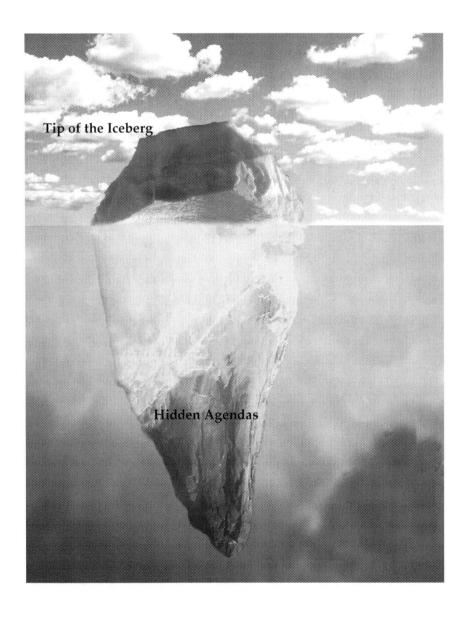

STRONGHOLD: A FORTIFIED FORTRESS WITH LEVELS OR LAYERS HIDING A WOUND

LEVEL C: The Tip of the Iceberg, the Surface, Symptoms, Smoke, and Fruits
> Facades, Masks
>Unreal self
>Manifestations of the hunger -addiction
>Eating disorders, dependency
>Co-dependency, rigidity
>False religion (without Christ/power)
>Emotions popping up
LEVEL B: Defense and Reactions Pride, fear, rebellion, hunger, control, domination, intimidation, witchcraft, unforgiveness, sinfulness, resentment, anger, wrath, retaliation, attack, judgment, condemnation, self-pity, self hate, self-loathing, rage, false protectors, survival, arrogance, keep walls up, splits, resistance
REPENTANCE
LEVEL A: The Core, Roots, Hidden Wounds, Place of Deepest Hurt Betrayal, loneliness, lack, loss, grief, abuse: mental, emotional, physical, sexual, lack, hopelessness, humiliation, rejection, abandonment, shame, little child hurt, little child captive, little child lost, lamentation, wailing, weeping, mourning, deep sadness
INNER HEALING: JESUS AT THE CORE

Jesus ministry is our commission

Mark 16:17b: Heal the Sick

Mark 16:17: Cast out devils

Acts 10:38 Heal those oppressed by the devil

Luke 4:18 Heal the brokenhearted; open prison doors and set captives free

We are going to follow this commission by bringing the panorama of the lies, death, and darkness to the Truth, Life, and Light of the ministry Jesus Christ. View the following chart recalling the picture of the Volcano and the three layers we listed: the core, reactions and defenses, and surface smoke. Recall the definition of stronghold.

To begin the process of healing, we ask the Holy Spirit to give us entrance, take us from the surface with its manifestations to the core, the place of deepest woundings. The spirit of a man is the lamp of the Lord, searching all the inner depths of his heart. (Proverbs 20:27)

He will lead us through the system of false identity, help us dismantle the structure of the false personality, expose the 'false self' (the old man) to us and the prayer recipient himself.

Our plan follows the chart above. We break barriers and defenses and go to the root. Level C identifies the surface areas. Level B identifies the middle areas with its defenses and reactions. Level A identifies the core.

We have to address the cement that holds the stronghold together.

(Always loosen the cement of unforgiveness)

1) Generational curses and demonization (Transmission of issues): Every unconfessed sin, i.e. the occult, occult societies, other religions, sexual immorality, abuse, abortion, etc.

C/R/R/F/B:

- Confess
- Repent
- Renounce
- Forgive
- Bless

2) Personal sin – occult, sexual, etc (as above)

C/R/R/F:

- Confess
- Repent
- Renounce
- Forgive

3) Trauma and reactions to trauma: Emotional wounding, memories, unforgiveness, shame, rejection – rebellion complex

4) Ungodly beliefs (UB): I am flawed, I am defective, I am unlovable, unworthy, it is my fault, everybody will reject me, abandon me, leave me

5) Inner vows (IV): heart of stone. I will never open up to anybody

6) Ignorance: Of the Word of God, of who I am in Christ, that my healing was already accomplished at the cross

7) Soul ties: inner soul ties, inner alliances with spirits within, outer soul ties

8) Familiar spirits of the personality, familiar spirits of the generations

9) Demonization (of levels A, B, C: infestation of the wound, infestation of the reactions and defenses, infestation of surface behaviors, i.e. addictions

10) Witchcraft: Control, manipulation, domination, intimidation, rebellion, stubbornness, bitterness, idolatry, iniquity (1 Samuel 15:23)

Prayer

There is a deep sadness under tons of rubble. We became dishonest to survive, we learned how to hide our pain, how to hide our shame. We became arrogant to survive. Today we take off the evil armor of false protection, we come bare before our Lord. It is Him who heals us, Jehova Rapha. We lay down our false weapons of war, we lay down our defenses. We lay down ourselves.

We appropriate the exchange

> We release the complete old man onto the cross

> We take on Jesus, He is the one who heals us

We go to the core

To the place of our deepest wound

Come Holy Spirit

Come Comforter

Come Spirit of Truth

Take me in

Take me to the core

Come Lord Jesus, come with me, to rescue that little child that has remained captive

The innocent

The pure

The vulnerable

The frail

The hurt inner child

So we go to the place of the deepest hurt

And we invite Jesus to be with us right there

We are the lamp of the Lord

We search the inward places

Abandonment, rejection, shame, hurt, betrayal, fear, loneliness, lack, lack of love, isolation, hopelessness

Jesus is ministering at the core. We break every lie of the devil implanted in our core:

It was our fault

We are unloved

We are flawed and defective

We bring the truth – Jesus, the Word into our depth. He has made us accepted in the beloved (Ephesians 1)

The river of life

The river of blessings

Flows inside

We forgive our offenders in a deeper way, from our heart

We forgive ourselves

We break all strongholds. We have mighty, divine, supernatural weapons to pull down strongholds. (2 Corinthians 10:4-5)

We have been sent over nations and the kingdoms to root out and to pull down, to destroy and to throw down, to build and to plant. (Jeremiah 1:10)

So this is what the Sovereign Lord says: " See I lay a stone in Zion, a tested stone, a precious cornerstone for a sure foundation; the one who trusts will never be dismayed." (Isaiah 28:16) NIV

The high praises of God are in our mouth and a two edged sword in our hands, to execute vengeance on the nations, and punishment on the peoples, to bind their kings with chains and their nobles with fetters of iron; to execute on them the written judgment, this honor have all His saints. Praise the Lord! (Psalms 149:6-9)

Behold I give you the authority to trample on serpents and scorpions and over all the power of the enemy, and nothing shall by any means hurt you. (Luke 10:19)

V11 In Him you were also circumcised with the circumcision made without hands, by putting off the body of the sins of the flesh, by the circumcision of Christ,

V12 buried with Him in baptism, in which you were also raised with Him through faith in the working of God, who raised Him from the dead

v13 And you, being dead in your trespasses and the uncircumcision of your flesh, He has made alive together with Him, having forgiven you all trespasses,

V14 having wiped out the handwriting of requirements that was against us, which was contrary to us. And He has taken it out of the way, having nailed it to the cross.

V15 Having disarmed principalities and powers, He made a public spectacle of them, triumphing over them in it. (Colossians 2)

We have the Word of God, the Sword of the Spirit.

V12 For the word of God is living and powerful, and sharper than any two-edged sword, piercing even to the division of soul and spirit, and of joints and marrow, and is a discerner of the thoughts and intents of the heart. V13 And there is no creature hidden from His sight, but all things are naked and open to the eyes of Him to whom we must give account. (Hebrews 4)

Jeremiah 23:29 – Is not my word like a fire, says the Lord, and like a hammer that breaks the rock in pieces.

Finally, we appropriate our commission:

Jeremiah 51:20 – You are my battle axe and weapons of war.

Job 22:28 – You will declare a thing and it will be established for you so light will shine on your ways.

Now we expel the enemy (Be sure to review the chapter on deliverance). We are going to cast out demons from the three levels. Evil spirits attached to unhealed wounds (Level A). Evil spirits of defenses and reactions such as pride, fear, control, bitterness, unforgiveness in level B are a major sinful part of the stronghold. Then the surface behaviors (level C) like addiction, codependency, flesh and world idolatry etc are also demonized. Here we can add our individual problems such as any illness, disease, infirmity, besetting sin etc. It is very practical to use the diagram of strongholds.

Our goal is a sanctified temple of spirit, soul and body (1Thessalonians 5:23).

1Thessalonians 5:24 – Faithful is He that calleth you, who will also do it!

Now we are to declare out loud:

A) I command out of me, with the power and authority invested to me by Jesus Christ and in the name of Jesus Christ, all root demons (Level A). Mention each one of them i.e. demons of hurt, demons of abuse, demons of rejection etc.

I command them to leave me now.

Take a deep breath and cough them out in the name of Jesus. Keep commanding them to come out. Send them to the feet of Jesus and command them never to return.

B) In the name of Jesus Christ I command out of me all spirits at level B, spirits of defenses, reactions, false protectors, walls, control, unforgiveness, bitterness, attack etc (See diagram of strongholds). I command them to leave me now.

Take a deep breath and cough them out in the name of Jesus. Keep commanding them to come out. Send them to the feet of Jesus and command them never to return.

C) In the name of Jesus I command out of me all surface demons, all smoke demons, addictions, co-dependencies, illnesses, pains etc.

I command them to leave me now.

Take a deep breath and cough them out, send them to the feet of Jesus and command them never to return.

After deliverance we must infill the whole house (you) with the Holy Spirit (see Matt 12:43,44). Invite the Holy Spirit to occupy every part of your body, i.e. head, mind, emotions, thoughts, eyes, ears, mouth. Every part and area of your body, every cell in your body.

Thank You Jesus.

Praise the Lord.

Then proclaim the blessings of your new life in Christ (1 Ephesians 1:3). Declare your new beliefs at all levels:

Level A – instead of rejection, acceptance in the Beloved. Instead of shame, double honor. Beauty for ashes, the oil of joy for mourning, the garment of praise for the spirit of heaviness etc.

Level B – Declare total forgiveness. Now we are under the control of the Spirit of God. God has not given us the spirit of fear, but the spirit of power, love and sound mind. We love God, love ourselves, love our neighbors.

Peace shalom. We depend on Him and totally trust Him.

Level C – We are not of the world. We don't live by the flesh. We live in the Spirit and walk in the Spirit. We are ambassadors of Christ. We proclaim the kingdom of God – we bring heaven into earth. We teach, preach, heal and deliver. We have become a blessing and we bless. The Lord has become our everlasting light and the days of our mourning have ended (Isaiah 60).

Amen.

CHAPTER EIGHT
"BABYLON"

1. Destroying Babylonian Strongholds

The father in Heaven ponders: why are my children so bereft? I gave them my child, my only child so they would have freedom. I am always sending fishermen and workers of the field and I send you today.

The spirit of the Lord is upon me because He has anointed me and qualified me to preach the good news (The Gospel) to the poor and afflicted. He hath sent me <u>to bind up and to heal</u> the broken-hearted. He has sent me <u>to preach, to announce and proclaim deliverance, release</u> the captives and <u>liberty</u> (Physical, emotional, mental, spiritual) and recovery of sight to the blind, to send forth as delivered, to set at liberty, to open prison doors of those who are downtrodden, bruised, crushed and broken down. To proclaim the accepted and acceptable year of the Lord, the day when salvation and the free favors of the Lord profusely abound. Luke 4:18-19

Today this scripture has been fulfilled while you are here present and hearing. Luke 4:21b

Rene Pelleya-Kouri, M.D.

Isaiah 61: 1-11

The Spirit of the Sovereign LORD is on me,
because the LORD has anointed me
to proclaim good news to the poor.
He has sent me to bind up the brokenhearted,
to proclaim freedom for the captives
and release from darkness for the prisoners,
to proclaim the year of the LORD's favor
and the day of vengeance of our God,
to comfort all who mourn,
and provide for those who grieve in Zion—
to bestow on them a crown of beauty
instead of ashes,
the oil of joy
instead of mourning,
and a garment of praise
instead of a spirit of despair.
They will be called oaks of righteousness,
a planting of the LORD
for the display of his splendor.

They will rebuild the ancient ruins
and restore the places long devastated;
they will renew the ruined cities
that have been devastated for generations.
Strangers will shepherd your flocks;
foreigners will work your fields and vineyards.
And you will be called priests of the LORD,
you will be named ministers of our God.
You will feed on the wealth of nations,
and in their riches you will boast.

Instead of your shame
you will receive a double portion,
and instead of disgrace

you will rejoice in your inheritance.
And so you will inherit a double portion in your land,
and everlasting joy will be yours.

For I, the LORD, love justice;
I hate robbery and wrongdoing.
In my faithfulness I will reward my people
and make an everlasting covenant with them.
Their descendants will be known among the nations
and their offspring among the peoples.
All who see them will acknowledge
that they are a people the LORD has blessed.

I delight greatly in the LORD;
my soul rejoices in my God.
For he has clothed me with garments of salvation
and arrayed me in a robe of his righteousness,
as a bridegroom adorns his head like a priest,
and as a bride adorns herself with her jewels.
For as the soil makes the sprout come up
and a garden causes seeds to grow,
so the Sovereign LORD will make righteousness
and praise spring up before all nations (NIV)

[Key Scripture Jeremiah 51]

Babylon Is:

Rebellious

Idolatry

Addicted to magic – witchcraft

Profane and sacrilegious

Wicked

Arrogant

Secure and self-confident

Grand and stately

Covetous

Oppressive

Cruel and destructive

King of Babylon

Besieges the city of God

Takes captives

Spoils the temple

Burns Jerusalem

Burns the temple of God

A type of antichrist

Perpetual desolation

Captivity

God is a destroying wind and spirit

We attack rebellious Babylon

He sends us tanners, winnowers that will tan or winnow her and empty her

We are the battle axe, the weapon of war, the spoilers, the winnowers.

We have the Word that is like fire and like a hammer, a fire that consumes all and a hammer that breaks into pieces the rock of most stubborn resistance. This is the time of the Lord's vengeance. He renders to her recompense. Babylon is fallen and shattered, destroyed. Let us declare in Zion the work of the Lord and God. His purpose concerning Babylon is to destroy it, for that is the vengeance of the Lord, the vengeance of His temple. The Lord has both purposed and done that which He spoke.

Babylon your end has come and the line measuring your life is cut and severed. 'The Lord of hosts has sworn by himself.' We have a song and a shout of victory over you. You who conquer Babylon are my battle axe. With you I break nations in pieces and destroy kingdoms, horse and rider, chariot and charioteer, governors and commanders.

Before your eyes I will do it. O destroying mountain I stretch my hand over you and make you a burnt out mountain. Oh Babylon you are waste and desolate forever. Set up a standard, blow the trumpet, prepare and dedicate yourselves for war. For the purposes of the Lord against Babylon stand – He makes that land desolate without habitation.

The warriors of Babylon become weak and helpless. Her dwelling places are burned up. Her defenses are broken down. Babylon is totally taken over. The inhabitants of Zion say "May the violence done to me and to my flesh and blood be avenged. Therefore, thus says the Lord, behold I will plead your cause and take vengeance for you.

I will dry up Babylon and Babylon shall become heaps of ruins, an astonishing desolation without an inhabitant. I will punish and execute judgment upon Bel and resave the captives.

Yes, the wall of Babylon has fallen. I will execute judgment upon Babylon's idols and images. My destroyers, spoilers, will destroy the stronghold of Babylon.

There is the sound of a cry and great destruction and ruin in the land of the Chaldeans, for the Lord is destroying Babylon and laying her to waste. The destroyer has come upon her. The broad walls of Babylon shall be utterly overthrown and the foundations made bare and her high gates shall be burned with fire. Babylon is cut off, nothing shall remain and dwell in it. It shall be desolate forever.

You are to bind a stone and cast it into the midst of the Euphrates then say, "thus will Babylon sink and not rise because of what I have done to her" says the Lord.

ᴡᶥ

CHAPTER NINE
"FIBROMYALGIA"

Physical illnesses remain a mystery. Great people of God at times do not get healed and sinners receive a miracle. We believe the Bible. All who came to Jesus got healed and He said "I do only what the Father wants me to do." He also said "If you believe in me you will do the same as I did and greater works." He gave us His Holy Spirit, the same one that gave Him the power to heal, so we are encouraged to seek the same results: healing.

We have seen God heal the body in myriad ways, places and times:

1. Through reading the Word, or praise and worship
2. Through laying on of hands
3. Through deliverance
4. Through forgiveness, or inner healing
5. Through a word of knowledge, or through prophecy
6. Through the gift of tongues
7. Through the fruit of the Spirit: Joy or Peace
8. In homes, in the streets, in churches
9. In the medical office, far away
10. In small and huge conferences
11. Immediately or slowly

12. At the moment of salvation
13. Before salvation
14. Through the giving of tithes and offerings
15. Through holy communion
16. Through confession
17. Through soaking in His presence
18. Through fasting and prayer
19. Through the ministry of angels etc.

Some of us have also been called to investigate root causes and the mechanisms of disease.

We have meditated upon the following scriptures to help us continue our quest.

Isaiah 5:13,14

V13 Therefore my people have gone into captivity. Because they have no knowledge, their honorable men are famished, and their multitude dried up with thirst.

V14 Therefore Sheol has enlarged itself and opened its mouth beyond measures. Their glory as their multitude and their pomp, and he who is jubilant, shall descend into it.

Psalms 20:27 – The spirit of man is the lamp of the Lord

Psalms 21:22 – A wise man scales the city of the mighty and brings down the trusted stronghold

Psalms 25:2 – It is the glory of God to conceal a matter, but the glory of kings is to search out a matter

Deuteronomy 29:29 – The secret things belong to the Lord our God, but those things which are revealed belong to us and to our children forever, that we may do the words of this law.

Isaiah 28:16-17

V16 Therefore thus says the Lord God "Behold, I lay in Zion a stone for a foundation, a tried stone, a precious cornerstone, a sure foundation; whoever believes will not act hastily.

V17 Also I will make justice the measuring line, and righteousness the plummet. The hail will sweep away the refuge of lies and the waters will overflow the hiding place.

Fibromyalgia could be considered as part of a group of illnesses that have strong psychosomatic components. We will use it as our example to pray for healing in this arena.

Investigating the root cause and dynamics of illnesses of this type could shed light into many other illnesses.

That could be a bold statement, but, historically, we have approached medicine in a purely scientific, mechanical way. The status of the spirit, soul, mind, feelings and emotions has NOT entered the examining room, or the medical history survey. The affect of hidden hurts and wounds remain under cover.

The group of illnesses that have been related to fibromyalgia include chronic fatigue syndrome, irritable bowel syndrome, temporomandibular joint disorders, multiple chemical sensitivities, tension and migraine headache, interstitial cystitis, localized and myofascial pain disorders.[8]

There are also many other illnesses that we could mention: ADHD, bulimia, dysthimia, anxiety, OCD (Obsessive Compulsive Disorder), panic, PTSD (Post Traumatic Stress Disorder), premenstrual dysphoric disorder, social phobia, asthma, some arthridites, depressive disorders, etc.

It is possible that God is showing us a way into healing that is applicable to most illnesses. We continue to follow the Holy Spirit's direction, as He knows the needs of each individual and promises to direct our path.

We are exploring possible causes for our sicknesses and ways to appropriate the healing that was already accomplished at the cross for us by our Lord.

Read and meditate on the following scriptures concerning healing: Isaiah 53:4,5, Matt 8:17, 1 Peter 2:24, Exodus 15:26, Psalm 107:20, Psalm 103:3, and any others you may find helpful. As you begin this process, read each passage with 'new' eyes, searching for truths unknown to you before. Ask the Holy Spirit for divine revelation concerning healing in each passage.

Panorama of Illnesses

Fibromyalgia

It is a stronghold

It is the principality

It is the strongman - it has armor

It has a history

It has underlings

It is a fortress

It has a core and it has layers

The following diagram illustrates the hidden wounds (inside circle) with the person in pain, represented by the outer circle:

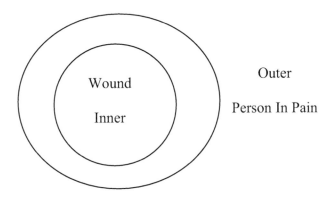

There is a person, a personality after the wound. The

personality of fibromyalgia.

The familiar spirit
The strongman
The principality
The fortress
The unfillable hole of unmet needs sinks the ship

Who is talking?

Familiar spirits talk out of the ground. (Isaiah 29:4)
Hell opens its mouth and takes us in. In our ignorance we remain captive. (Isaiah 5:13) Splits, hidden places hold us down. We live in the land of rejection and despair.

I need to be loved
Any love suffices = wrong love, sinful love
Hell enlarges its mouth
Ignorance of our victory in Christ keeps us captive

Sin begets sin, begets sin, begets sin
Our only solution is Jesus
We have to raise up in standard that will fill the whole house, spirit, soul, and body

There is a story to the person in pain. How was that reality created, formed, concocted? How did the person in pain come about? Layer, after layer, after layer, it was created. Sin begins the whole ordeal, the wounds and evil spirits take over.

I. Sins of the generations
    Transference of the appropriate circumstances
    Transfer of the potential
    Early wounds and hurt

II. The Wound
    The Creation of the Wound
    The trauma
    The core

This diagram represents the wound itself containing all the core issues

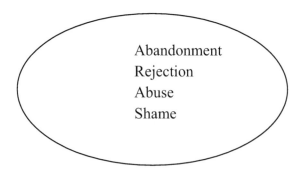

Abandonment
Rejection
Abuse
Shame

Proverbs 25:28 – Spirit out of control, broken down walls
(= entrance doors!)

These are reactions to the wound
Progressive building of the fortress
The layers of the onion

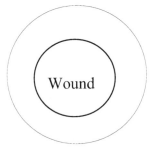

Defenses
Resistance
Denial
Repression
Reactions

There are different manifestations in the wound, reactions to the wound and outer manifestations

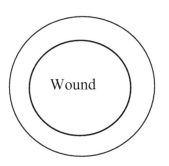

Unforgiveness
Bitterness
Resentment
Violence
Self-pity
Self-hate
Rebellion
Control

The Outward Manifestations of this woundedness can include many of the following:

A) seeking 'love' in all the wrong places ending in addictions of all kinds

B) Mechanisms of self hatred (revealing loss of our intended identity in Christ)

C) Finally manifesting sickness in the body (fibromyalgia and other diseases)

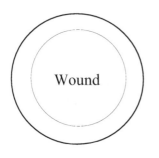

Outer Manifestations
a) Seeking love in wrong places
Addictions
Love addiction
Codependecy

b) Sicknesses
Fibromyalgia

Mechanisms in self-hate.

Sin opens the door.

Sin leads to death- diseases
        illnesses
        infirmities
        pain
        suffering
        afflictions

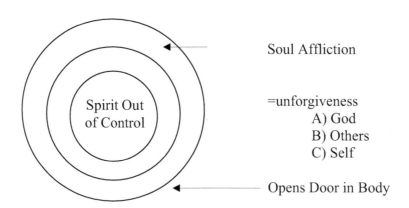

Soul Affliction

=unforgiveness
    A) God
    B) Others
    C) Self

Opens Door in Body

We are made in the image of God. If you hate yourself, you hate God, you hate others, you are breaking the first commandment.

Self-hate = self-attack.

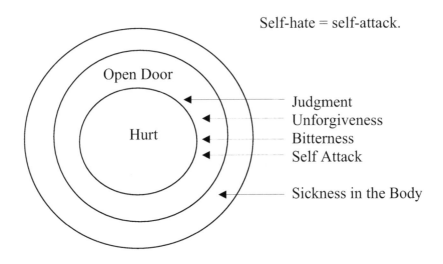

Open Door

Hurt

Judgment
Unforgiveness
Bitterness
Self Attack

Sickness in the Body

Spiritual   Mental/
                 Emotional   —   Physical

Self-attack can alter the immune system: cells respond. There is a spiritual authority in us that rules over the soul. The soul rules over the body. The whole system is perverse.

Isaiah 1:5,6,7
V5 Why should we be stricken again?
You will revolt more and more
The whole head is sick and the whole heart faints

V6 From the sole of the foot even to the head
There is no soundness in it
But wounds and bruises and putrefying sores;
They have not been closed or bound up,
or soothed with ointment
V7 Your country is desolate
Your cities are burned with fire;
Strangers devour your land in your presence
and it is desolate as overthrown by strangers

The whole head is sick, we have been invaded.

Jeremiah 51:51 – We are ashamed because we have heard reproach
Shame has covered our faces
For strangers have come into the sanctuaries of the Lord's house

We must reach and heal the core:

1. Repent and renounce the sins of the generations sexual, abortions, abuses and traumas, the occult, all sins

2. Repent of our sins – as above plus: Fear, unforgiveness, self-hate, judgements, bitterness, depression, unbelief, rebellion… Forgive all offenders

3. Go to the core for healing
    Invite Jesus to heal every trauma

4. Change ungodly beliefs
    Believe the Word of God
    Appropriate who you are in Christ, i.e. instead of rejection and worthlessness proclaim that you are accepted in the Beloved; Instead of shame receive God's double honor for you.

5. Repent and renounce inner vows
   Break the stronghold of the heart of stone
   Receive the new heart – Ezekiel 11:19, 18:31, 36:24-38
   Receive love and trust

6. Repent and renounce inner and outer soul ties
   Inner soul ties: alliances with evil, survival defense mechanisms, evil reactions and resistances, rebellion and stubbornness
   Outer soul ties: with any individual with whom you have an unholy relationship

7. Cleanse your temple (review Deliverance chapter)
   Renew your relationship with Jesus
   Declare Him as your Lord and Savior
   Confess, repent and renounce all of the above conditions, i.e. fear, depression, self-hate, bitterness, unforgiveness…
   Bind the spirit of fibromyalgia and its defenses and underlings (All of the above)
   Command them all to leave you, command the pain to go, in the name of Jesus command them never to return

8. Spend time filling your whole house (yourself), with the Holy Spirit: Spirit, soul, body, muscles, bones, immune system, organs, cells,
   Thank and praise God for your healing

We have seen many people totally and permanently healed from fibromyalgia with a short deliverance prayer such as this one. Amen.

CHAPTER TEN
"LAST THOUGHTS"

You act on the One who waits for you.
You meet Him who rejoices and does righteousness.
Rend the heavens.
Come down.
Shake the mountains.
I stir myself up to take hold of you.
I am Your people.
You are my Father.
Mighty rivers shower into earth.
There is a river whose streams shall make glad the city of God.
The flowing river of His presence.
The anointing of our God.
Roaring waters.
His voice is heard as a mighty thunder.
The King comes in His majesty.
Glorious Son of the Father.
The white horse with the King of Kings.
His sword of righteousness destroys our enemies.
We bow and ride our horses behind Him.
Angels blow hard on their shofars.
The winds of heaven also come.
Holy Spirit rumbles.

The wind that shakes our houses.
We have deep foundations in the cornerstone.
We rejoice in such shakings.
Oil erupts.
We are full of oil.
There is fire in our midst.
Our bones burn.
We have to speak the Word of God.
We move forward.
There is no backward movement.
Each step forward increases our anointing.
Sanctification rises.
The fire consumes us.
We cry holy and sing with the angels.
We throw down our crowns with the elders.
Creatures soar in our midst.
We receive eyes of revelation.
We can see in the spirit.
We see the things of God.
We see what the Father is doing.
The wind takes us wherever it wants to.
We go with the flow and do the things of God.
We truly have been taken out of captivity and placed in the Kingdom of God.
God is in our midst.
He rules in our lives.
We really love it.
The old has passed away.
We are the new creation born for relationship.
I embrace Jesus and never let Him go.
He loved me first and gave Himself for me.
We both died on the cross and were resurrected.
I sit in heavenly places with my King.
He has given me all blessings in heavenly places in Christ.
Oh my God I am so happy.
I am so full of joy.

I am so near you.
My heart exalts you.
I praise you, Lord of lords, King of kings.
Messiah.
Emanuel.
God with me.
Thank you Lord for You.
You are the absolute goodness that came into my life.
You are reaching the lost me.
Your presence has changed me in such a way that I can now love.
Lord you are love.
You infuse me with Your love.
You share with me Your garment of love.
I have received Your blessings and now I bless.
You gave to us and now we are givers.
Hallelujah.
It is a never ending flowing in-filling river from the throne.
The gospel of healing is in the river.
The Word of God from beginning to end is in the waters.
I am taken by the river.
I jump in the river and enter the currents of God.
Mighty God infuses me with power.
Every part of me shakes in His presence.
I am for Him and He is for me.
An army is raised in the presence.
We hold on to the presence.
We are anointed with fresh oil.
My horn is exalted like a wild ox.
I come out of the barn leaping in joy.
Oh, to do the things of the King.
He placed the kingdom within me.
He placed his Spirit within me.
I am a witness now and go to all the world.
Revival fire is in my heart and I set places on fire.
Thank you Jesus that I like what You like.

I do like You do.

I go where You go.

It's only you Lord, only You.

My ways are bathed in butter and oil flows continuously from the rock.

The lion roars and the nations submit.

The enemy was disarmed a long time ago.

We receive revelation of our victory.

Everything is in Christ.

We destroy the lies of Satan.

We are not down but up.

We move through trials, tribulations, temptations (we have been equipped).

We receive love in our hearts and a crown of life.

Hallelujah.

There are always new territories to move into, inside when we soak, outside when He conquers.

Many who were in prisons now wear the mark of righteousness.

Thank You Lord.

The never ending river of God continues to flow.

Daily we gather the lost and bring them to the house of God.

They become houses of God and soon bring others to the King.

The whole world rejoices.

The conquering light and the conquering glory are taking over.

The kingdom of God rules.

Forever and ever.

Amen

APPENDIX[9]

How to keep your deliverance

Demonic groupings

Final checkup

Teach them how to keep their freedom:
Because demons will try to return, we must tell people how to keep them out. They must be filled with the Holy Spirit an hold onto the new land God has given them, noting how God gave the land, formerly held by their enemies, to the Israelites:

"Little by little I will drive them out before you, until you have increased enough to take possession of the land." (Ex. 23:30)

People must be taught how to keep the new ground we help them acquire because the enemy will try to take it back. So, they should only receive as much deliverance at one time as we can reasonably do in one session remembering that we must also teach them how to keep demons from reentering them. Most of the following provisions are discussed at length in chapter 7 of Frank Marzullo's book "Eight Keys to Spiritual and Physical Health".

1. Total commitment to Christ. (Matt. 22:37, John 12:26) Unless a person is totally surrendered to Christ as Lord, he will continue to experience problems due to being lead by his flesh. Demons prey on such people who fail to deny their self-life. Those who embrace the cross, considering their sinful nature dead with Christ, defeat the power of sin and mental problems. (Matt. 10:38 and 16:24, Luke 9:23 and 14:26, Phil 3:17-19, Rom 5:10).

2. Remembering that obedience is better than sacrifice, obey God instead of engaging in works to please Him. (Heb 4:9-11)

3. Be accountable to someone to watch over your life. (Heb 13:7 and 17, 1 Thes. 5:12)

4. Regularly study and draw life from the Word of God. (Ps. 1:1-3, Ps. 119:9, 11, 105 and 165)

5. Put on and wear the full armor of God, standing strong in the power of His might. (Eph. 6:10-18)

6. Pray in all circumstances: thanksgiving, praise, and worship. (1 Thes. 5:17, Ps. 100)

7. Keep in fellowship with spiritually-minded people. (Heb. 10:24-25)

8. Regularly make positive confessions of faith in God's ability and power which is working in you. (Mark 11:22-24, Rom 10:8-10)

9. Remember Luke 10:19. "I have given you authority to trample on snakes and scorpions and to overcome all the power of the enemy; nothing will harm you. All demons are powerless as you abide in Christ's victory.

10. Don't be yoked with unbelievers. (1 Cor. 6:11-7:1)

11. Memorize and understand your position in Christ. Zech. 3:1-3 and 7, Gal. 2:20)

12. Deal promptly with sin. (Isa. 59:2, 1 John 1:9)

13. Forgive and forget. (Matt. 6:14-15, 7:1-2, 18:15-35, Heb. 10:17)

14. Keep home life in order, or restore it to divine order. (1 Tim. 3:3-13, Eph. 5:18-33, 6:1-4)

15. Submit yourself to God. Resist the devil, and he will flee from you. Submitting everything in our lives to God must precede resisting the devil and seeing him flee. James 4:7)

Demonic groupings

Demons are commonly encountered in the following groupings:

Resentment
Bitterness, destruction, hatred (various kinds), unforgiveness, violence, temper, anger, retaliation, murder

Self-will
Rebellion, stubbornness, disobedience, anti-submissiveness, egotism

Contention
Strife, bickering, argument, quarreling, fighting, criticism

Control
Possessiveness, dominance, witchcraft, Jezebel, Ahab, Mama's boy/girl

Retaliation
Destruction, spite, hatred, sadism, hurt, cruelty, mutilation, revenge

Accusation
Judging, criticism, fault finding, finger pointing

Rejection
Fear of rejection, self-rejection, isolationism, escapism

Insecurity
Inferiority, self-pity, loneliness, timidity, shyness, inadequacy, ineptness, jealousy, rejection

Jealousy
Envy, suspicion, distrust, selfishness, hatred

Withdrawal
Pouting, daydreaming, fantasy, pretension, unreality, rejection, escapism

Escape
Indifference, stoicism, passivity, sleepiness, alcohol, drugs, silence

Passivity
Funk, indifference, listlessness, lethargy, laziness

Loneliness
Depression, despair, despondency, discouragement, defeatism, dejection, hopelessness, suicide, death, insomnia, morbidity, heaviness, gloom, burden, disgust, death wish

Worry
Anxiety, fear, dread, apprehension, timidity

Nervousness
Tension, headache, nervous habits, restlessness, excitement, insomnia, roving

Sensitiveness
Self-awareness, fear of man, fear of disapproval, retaliation

Persecution
Unfairness, fear of judgment, fear of condemnation, fear of accusation, fear of reproof, sensitiveness

Mental Illness
Insanity, madness, mania, retardation, senility, schizophrenia, paranoia, hallucinations

Schizophrenia
Paranoia

Paranoia
Jealousy, envy, suspicion, distrust, persecution, fears, confrontation

Confusion
Frustration, incoherence, forgetfulness

Doubt
Unbelief, self-delusion, skepticism

Indecision
Procrastination, compromise, confusion, forgetfulness, indifference

Self-deception
Self-seduction, pride, self-pity

Mind-binding
Confusion, fear of man, fear of failure, occult spirits, spiritism spirits

Mind idolatry
Intellectualism, rationalization, pride, ego

Fears (all kinds)
Phobias (all kinds), hysteria

Fear of authority
Lying, deceit, fear of man

Pride
Ego, vanity, self-righteousness, haughtiness, importance, judging, arrogance

Affectation
Theatrics, playacting, sophistication, pretension

Covetousness
Stealing, kleptomania, materialism, greed, discontent

Perfection
Pride, vanity, ego, frustration, criticism, judgment, irritability, intolerance, anger

Competition
Driving, argument, pride, ego

False Burden
False responsibility, false compassion, religious

Impatience
Agitation, frustration, intolerance, resentment, criticism

Grief
Sorrow, heartache, heartbreak, crying, sadness, cruelty

Fatigue
Tiredness, weariness, laziness

Infirmity
(any sickness or disorder)

Inheritance
(Physical), (emotional), (mental), (curses)

Death
Suicide, death wish

Hyperactivity
Restlessness, driving, pressure

Cursing
Blasphemy, coarse jesting, gossip, criticism, backbiting, mockery, belittling, railing

Addictive and Compulsive
Nicotine, alcohol, drugs, medications, caffeine, gluttony

Gluttony
Nervousness, compulsive eating, resentment, frustration, idleness, self-pity, self-reward, self-accusation, self-hatred, self-condemnation, indulgence, obesity

Guilt
Condemnation, unworthiness, embarrassment

Sexual Impurity
Lust, fantasy lust, masturbation, homosexuality, lesbianism, adultery, fornication, incest, Moab, Chemosh, harlotry, rape, exposure, frigidity, Incubus (male spirit), Succubus (female spirit), voyeurism (peeping Tom)

Cults
Hari-Krishna, Jehovah's witnesses, Christian Science, Rosicrucianism, Theosophy, Urantia, Subud, Latihan, Unity, Mormonism, Bahaism, Unitarianism

(Lodges, societies and social agencies using the Bible and God as a basis but omitting the blood atonement of Jesus) Freemasons

Occult
Ouija board, palmistry, handwriting analysis, automatic handwriting, ESP, hypnotism, horoscope, astrology, levitation, fortune telling, water witching, tarot cards, pendulum, witchcraft, black magic, white magic, conjuration, incantation, charms, channeling, fetishes, Santeria, spirits associated with (?), horror movies, astral projection, fortune cookies, reading tea leaves, New Age, cannibalism, mutilation, self-mutilation, Satanism, Dungeons & Dragons, acid rock music, Reiki

Religious
Ritualism, formalism, legalism, doctrinal obsession, doctrinal error, seduction, fear of God, fear of hell, fear of lost salvation, religiosity, judgment

Spiritism
Séance, spirit guide, necromancy, spiritism

False religions
Buddhism, Taoism, Hinduism, Islam, Shintoism, Confucianism, error, anti-christ, mockery, New Age

Final Checkup:

At the end of ministering to a large group of people, that is, mass deliverance, the Holy Spirit often leads us to go from head to toe as a final checkup. We believe that evil spirits often dwell in various parts of the body. We have seen many deliverances and healings by this way of praying. We instruct the group to place their hands on the area of their body that we are dealing with and to repeat the following:

HEAD – I command every spirit in my head to leave that causes: Strokes, Brain damage, Cancer, Tumors, Cysts, Blood clots, Epilepsy, Meningitis, Alzheimer's disease, Psychoses of all kinds, Schizophrenia, Paranoia, Phobias of all kinds,

Doublemindedness, Retardation, Senility, Hallucinations, Manias, Madness, Confusion, Forgetfulness, Frustration, Procrastination, Mind-binding, Bondage, Worry, Fear, Dread, Anxiety, Stress, Pressure, Occult spirits, Spiritism, Satanism, Nightmares, Migraines, Headaches, Mental torment, Suicide, and (name your own torment or other problem in your head). Come out in the name of Jesus.

After casting out all these demons, we then pray for the healing of that part of the head in the name of Jesus.

EYES (hands on eyes) – I command out every spirit in my eyes that causes: Blindness, Cataracts, Glaucoma, Floaters, Nearsightedness, Farsightedness, Lazy eye, Crossed eyes, Dry eyes, All other diseases and weaknesses of the eyes, Lust of the eyes, Pornography, Evil eye, Witchcraft, (name your own problem). Come out in the name of Jesus. Now speak to your eyes: Eyes be healed in Jesus name.

EARS (hands on ears) – I command out every spirit in my ears that causes: Deafness, Ringing in the ear, Ear aches, Ear infections, Inner ear problems, Meniere's syndrome, Loss of balance, Confusion, Spiritual deafness, Lying spirits, Spirits of error, (Name your own ear problem). Out in the name of Jesus. Now proclaim: Ears be healed in Jesus' name.

NOSE (hands on nose) – I command out every spirit in my nose that causes: Loss of smelling, Bloody nose, Post nasal drip, Sinusitis, Polyps, Breathing difficulties, (Name your own problem). Out in the Name of Jesus. Now say: Nose be healed in Jesus' name.

MOUTH (hands on mouth) – I command out every spirit in my mouth that causes: Gum infection, Tooth decay, Cavities, Bad bite, Jaw locking, Grinding of teeth, Canker sores, Lip sores, Loss of taste, Bad breath, Pyorrhea, Stuttering, Dumbness, Oral sex, Serpent spirits, Lying spirits, Swearing, Blasphemy, Dirty stories, Gossip, Blabbermouth. I command out of me all spirits of addiction: Alcohol, Wine, Beer, Drugs, Tobacco, Gluttony, (name your own). Come out in the name of Jesus. Now command: Mouth be healed in Jesus' name.

THROAT (hands on throat) – I command out every spirit in my throat that causes: Colds, Viruses, Thyroid, Goiters, Laryngitis, Swollen glands, Polyps, Tonsillitis, Malfunctioning of the epiglottis and my vocal cords, (name your problem). Out in the name of Jesus. Now say: Throat be healed in Jesus' name.

BONES, NECK, BACK AND JOINTS (one hand on back of neck, other hand on lower back) – I command out every spirit in my neck, back and joints, that causes: Pain, Crippling, Sway back, Curvature of the spine, Rheumatoid arthritis, Arthritis, Bursitis, Multiple sclerosis, I command out any spirit that affects my spinal cord, my nervous system, my back bone, my vertebrae, my bone marrow, (name your own problem). Come out in the name of Jesus. Now say: Neck, back, bones, and joints, be healed in Jesus' name.

ARMS, LEGS, KNEES, ANKLES, FEET (hands on the area that concerns you) – I command out every spirit in my *Name area that has difficulty*: Burning feet, cramps, Muscle spasms, Pain, Arthritis, Gout, Crippling, Water in the knee, Poor circulation, Ingrown toe nails, Fungus, Spurs, Warts, Corns, Bunions, Fallen arches, Swollen feet or ankles, (name your own problem). Out in the name of Jesus. Now say to your limbs: be healed in Jesus' name.

CHEST AREA (hands on chest) – I command out every spirit in my chest area that causes: All heart problems and lung problems: Abnormal blood pressure, Irregular heart beat, Enlarged heart, Breast cancer, Tumors, Growths, Cysts, Emphysema, Respiratory problems, (name your problem), out in the name of Jesus. Now pray: Chest area be healed in Jesus' name.

ABDOMINAL AREA AND PELVIS (hands on abdominal area and pelvis) – I command out every spirit in my abdominal area that causes: Malfunctions and problems in my: Liver, Spleen, Intestines, Pancreas, Bladder, Kidneys, Urinary tract, Small and large bowels, and Reproductive organs, including spirits that want to give me cancer in these organs. I command out of me spirits of: Hemorrhoids, Diverticulitis, Endometriosis, Ovarian Cysts, Ulcers, Crohn's Disease, Impotency, Barrenness, (name any other problem), I command you all to come out in the name of Jesus. Now say: body, be healed in Jesus' name.

[We have often found that spirits of lust and witchcraft take over the reproductive organs. We have commanded out in Jesus' name covens of witches that were in women, warlock spirits that were in some men.]

GENERAL, SYSTEMIC PROBLEMS (hands on any particular area of concern) – I command out of me spirits that cause: Cancers, Lupus, Skin diseases, Vascular diseases, Clogged arteries, Unbalanced blood cell count, Varicose veins, Shingles, Immune deficiency diseases (such as AIDS, ARC), Leukemia, Hodgkin's Disease, Lymphomas, Anemia, Problems in my lymphatic system, (name yours). Come out in the name of Jesus. Now say: Be healed in Jesus' name.

Name yourself and say, as you place hands on yourself from head to toe, "Be healed from head to toe. And precious Holy Spirit, please come into me, take the place of all these spirits we have cast out, and fill me from head to toe with all of You." Amen.

Praise God from whom all blessings flow...

References

[1]Wilkerson, D. (2005). Knowing God By Name: Names of God That Bring Hope and Healing. Grand Rapids, MI: Chosen Books.

[2]Frank Marzullo, T. S. (2006). *A Manual For the Deliverance Worker.* Florida: Frank Marzullo.

[3]MacNutt, F. (1995). *Deliverance From Evil Spirits: A Practical Manual.* Michigan: Chosen Books.

[4]Pelleya-Kouri, R. (2009). *Praying Doctors: Jesus in the Office.* BC Canada: Trafford Publishing.

[5]Prince, D. (1998). *They Shall Expel Demons: What You Need To Know About Demons- Your Invisible Enemies.* Michigan: Chosen Books.

[6]Miller, E. (2008). Deliver Us From Evil. Abbotsford, BC: Destiny Encounters.

[7]Collins, C. (2012, March 11). *Of Icebergs and Extended Content.* Retrieved July 2012, from Folded Story: Storytelling and Independent Publishing: http://foldedstory.com/2012/03/11/of-icebergs-and-extended-content/

[8] American Journal of Medicine, December 2009, Vol 122, No 12A

[9]Frank Marzullo, T. S. (2006). *A Manual For the Deliverance Worker.* Florida: Frank Marzullo.

Cheryl Williams
Healing Words Ministries, Inc.
September 10, 2015

ᴎ

FOREWORD

What a Joy to see this work completed! It has been a privilege to co-labor with Dr. Rene on this project. He operated much like Jesus, carrying the heavy load, allowing me the lighter burden and the easier yoke.

Several years ago, Dr. Rene and I met on the campus of Christian Healing Ministries in Jacksonville, Fl. I was employed by the MacNutts as the coordinator of Prayer Ministers, and as such, had many hands on experience with the students enrolled in the School of Healing Prayer. Dr. Rene was a zealous student seeking and Loving His Jesus with a hunger and thirst that has reached its promised fulfillment! Over the years our relationship has morphed from teacher/student to mentor/mentee and finally to brother and sister in Christ. We have fluidly exchanged places until now. We now recognize and honor Christ in each of us, Who continues to be Our Eternal Hope.

I came to Christian Healing Ministries as a prayer recipient, and was compelled to enroll as a student, and recognized my life's calling as I was mentored by the MacNutts and the staff there. When the opportunity came to join the staff, I was catapulted from student to trainer and beyond! So many experiences at conferences and schools, and day to day ministry opportunities presented themselves until I realized I had become a trusted teacher/trainer and mentor for many.

I was honored when Dr. Rene invited me to speak at a gathering in Miami, and further humbled at the completion of his first book, when he invited ME to write comments for its publication. By then I had seen how the Lord powerfully rewarded this man's daily search for Him with teachings, visions and prophecies for himself AND the body of Christ. His books are a product of these times.

When he shared that he had been given material to write a book on Inner Healing, I eagerly asked and was granted permission to participate. Given my extensive experience in inner healing prayer, and my love for teaching, I was excited to partner with Dr. Rene and the Holy Spirit to produce a work I knew would change the 'playing field' for those of us who so eagerly await His appearing in the lives of those to whom we minister.

As the title indicates, this work helps us navigate our way from places of despair and hopelessness into the marvelous Light of Truth in Christ Jesus, Our Hope. The Lord has used Dr. Rene to help us as we seek our own healing from the pits of shame, AND to minister powerfully to those who cross our paths seeking freedom and truth. I pray many lives will be radically transformed as a result of God's faithfulness to us and Dr. Rene's faithfulness to Our Lord.

Printed in the United States
By Bookmasters